SCHOOL
COUNSELING
Problems and Methods

ROBERT D. MYRICK
JOE WITTMER

University of Florida
Gainesville, Florida

 GOODYEAR PUBLISHING COMPANY, INC.

Pacific Palisades, California

Goodyear Education Series

Theodore W. Hipple, *Editor*
UNIVERSITY OF FLORIDA

Popular Media and the Teaching of English
THOMAS R. GIBLIN

School Counseling: Problems and Methods
ROBERT MYRICK AND JOE WITTMER

Secondary School Teaching: Problems and Methods
THEODORE W. HIPPLE

Elementary School Teaching: Problems and Methods
MARGARET KELLY GIBLIN

This volume is dedicated to
Mary Jean and Sue
and to our children
Mark, Susan, and Karen
&
Diane, Scott, and David

CONTENTS

42121

PREFACE

Guidance services have a special place in our schools. These services represent society's concern for the individual. Guidance has developed in no other country to the extent that it has in American schools. This is due in part to the democratic philosophy that embraces our country and our belief in respect for individuals and their differences.

During the past decade, the school counselor has become firmly established in most secondary schools. Counseling came into existence in order to help students to understand themselves and to review alternatives available to them. Today counselors perform a different role from that of teachers or administrators. Like all educators they are interested in facilitating individual growth and development, and are faced with problems that need to be resolved before they can be fully effective in their work.

There have been many books written on the subject of counseling. These books range in scope from what counseling is, what should be done, to who should receive counseling and when. Some books have specialized in particular aspects of the guidance function, such as organizational procedures or counseling theory. Students studying school counseling review theoretical positions and attempt to understand the role of the counselor, but they frequently comment that there is little value in theoretical problems until some counseling experience has been gained. When a person is abruptly confronted with an actual counseling situation, only then are his skills put to the test. For all counselors, this is the moment of truth. It is a time when they must act, for better or for worse.

Unfortunately, counseling theory and role definition too often only become meaningful after students have gained experience and met with a number of problems which call for a conceptualized rationale. Counselor educators have been confronted with the question of which comes first: experience or counseling theory? Or, perhaps they should be concurrent. How can counselor educators provide their students with situations that call for them to put into practice counseling theory, without endangering or risking the welfare of a counselee? It seemed to us that one of the best ways would be to study and work with some of the problems that counselors typically face when working in the school setting.

This text is a book of problems and methods. It is intended for use by prospective or relatively inexperienced counselors. However, even experienced counselors will find value in working out the problems. They provided them with the opportunity to examine their own solutions and positions in various situations and to explore their rationales about counseling. This book will also be helpful to teachers who are seeking to understand the role of the counselor. While teachers are not expected to serve two roles, some of the problems and solutions found in this book may provide insight. Likewise, the book will prove helpful to administrators as they attempt to understand the role of the counselor. While it is most likely that this book will find its way to beginning counselors in counselor education courses, it is possible that it could be useful for in-service workshops where experienced counselors and teachers work together to understand one another's roles and to develop new approaches in working with students.

Many of our best methods of working with people, either on a developmental or crisis basis, have come from working through a problem. In solving a problem values and theories are put to the test. After finding a solution to a problem, it is possible for a teacher or counselor to confirm or change his own professional theory and approach.

After studying the general field of counseling, it was decided that a profitable study would be a representative sample of problems in five basic areas. These include the counselor as counselor, consultant, manager of guidance services, co-worker, and cooperating member of a community. Each area represents a particular chapter or a theme area of problems in school counseling. All the problems included in this book are those that have actually been encountered by the authors, either in their own school counseling experiences, or as a result of consulting with school counselors.

The cases included in this text are designed as a four page unit. Each unit begins with a statement of the problem on the initial page. A blank facing page is next on which the reader can write his responses or describe how he would solve the problem and why he thinks his approach would be effective. The third page—again blank—allows the reader to write his reactions to the alternate solutions presented to him on the fourth page. There has been no attempt to arrange the solutions in a particular order nor assure the reader that all possibilities have been presented. Rather a few possible solutions have been offered in a random order so that they will stimulate the reader to explore several possibilities.

In each chapter after a series of problems, there follows a brief discussion that deals with the general topic of the chapter. The discussions are not meant to be comprehensive statements on the subject areas. Their aim is to give general overviews of the topics and to stimulate interest in the areas. Each chapter concludes with a short, basic reference section which will help the reader to find other approaches, ideas, and methods.

Students today at all levels are sending out the cry for relevancy. They are no longer interested in exploring ideas that have little or no meaning for their work or existence. Every college instructor faces the test of answering the students' question, "Is it really relevant to what I will be doing?" The authors believe that educators and students will find this text to be a stimulus for discussion of issues that are relevant today. In some respects, the problems represent a simulated experience for the readers. It is our hope that as beginning counselors examine the daily practice of functioning counselors, their own programs of preparation will become more meaningful, and this in turn will lead to the improvement of counseling in the schools.

Many people provided the inspiration and encouragement for the authors to write this book. While it is impossible to name all of these people, special thanks are extended to our colleagues in the Department of Counselor Education at the University of Florida and to Dr. Ted Hipple, who provided the initial encouragement and support. A special debt is owed to our counseling colleagues and students, both past and present, who helped us gain the experiences upon which this book is based. Special thanks are extended to Mrs. Jane Taylor and Mrs. Nanci Clyatt for typing the manuscript. Finally, we greatly appreciate the love, understanding, and sacrifices made by our families during the writing of this book.

CHAPTER ONE

The Counselor as a Counselor

TRUTH OR CONSEQUENCES

Brenda is an attractive 16-year-old junior at Newberry High School. It's difficult to remember all your students by name, but Brenda stood out because she had expressed so much thoughtful interest in someday becoming a dental hygienist.

She had been waiting to see you, and you invited her in. As you closed the door behind you, Brenda began talking—as if she had been prepared to blurt out her thoughts. "Well, I've got a problem. I've been thinking about it day and night. I can't tell my parents because they'd be so upset. I don't know what would happen if they knew. My mother will just die! You're the only person I can think of to talk to. You see, I think I'm pregnant."

It had been a long day, but suddenly you were alert. There was something about that phrase "I think I'm pregnant" that made you flinch inside. You had been trained not to show alarm when someone expressed a problem, and you even called on the standard phrase "Do you want to talk about it?" Brenda nodded, lifted her head, took a deep breath, and began her story, while you became the empathic listener. She told of the boy, her mother's dislike of him, and how her parents had tried to break up the relationship. Her parents had very high expectations for her. It was not easy for Brenda to talk with her parents, especially her mother.

As time passed, Brenda relaxed and apparently used your understanding help to look at facts, feelings, and what might lie ahead. The session ended with the scheduling of another appointment. As you left the office that night, you reminded yourself to consult with Mrs. Jones, the senior counselor.

However, that evening you received a telephone call from Brenda's mother. She said, "Brenda told me today that she had a serious talk with you. I know something is bothering her, but she says she doesn't want to talk. From what I gather, she told you about it. Frankly, I'm going out of my mind about Brenda and I'd like to know what's bothering her, so I can help. How does she expect me to help, if she won't talk with me? Please, tell me, what's wrong?"

Suddenly there is silence and it's your turn to talk. What do you say?

YOUR SOLUTION

YOUR REACTIONS TO THE ALTERNATE SOLUTIONS

ALTERNATE SOLUTIONS

1. Stall for time. Tell her that you don't usually receive calls about students at night, and ask if she could call tomorrow at school.

2. Tell her that Brenda may have a difficult problem. Hint that she will need to have a medical checkup, but avoid discussing anything else regarding the matter.

3. Tell her you'd like to talk about the matter, but not over the telephone. Make an appointment for the parents to see you the next day.

4. Ask to speak with Brenda. When she comes to the phone inquire as to "what's up?"

5. Report that you saw Brenda, at her request. Say you are sorry, but you cannot talk about the counseling session until the girl gives you permission to do so.

6. Offer reasurrance that in the near future the girl probably will be talking to the mother about various matters, and advise the mother to be understanding.

7. Deny that you talked with Brenda about anything serious.

8. Tell her that you have been caught by surprise and are busy at the moment (collecting your thoughts, of course) and will call her back.

TO SIR WITH LOVE . . .

You remember the time your college professor discussed the topic "Love, Sex, and Counseling." You recall the emphasis he placed on the powerful impact you could have on some students because of the special skills you were learning. He said, "Students need to experience empathic, warm, and interested listeners. It's a positive experience. However, there will be times when a student will misinterpret your intentions and become infatuated. They might even 'fall in love' with you because you seem so understanding."

You look at the note again. You're thinking that this can't be happening to you, but the words speak for themselves.

At first I thought you were meeting with me because you were just doing your job as a counselor. I realize now that you *really do care* about me—what happens to me. Yesterday I could see it in your eyes. You must be feeling the same loving feelings for me that I have for you. The thought of it sorta scares me, but it also draws me closer to you and I know you will understand when I say I thought of you in English class when we read the words of Kipling:

> None so true as you and I
> Sing the Lover's Litany:
> Love like ours can never die.
>
>   Yours,
>
>   D. S.

What now, counselor?

YOUR SOLUTION

YOUR REACTIONS TO THE ALTERNATE SOLUTIONS

ALTERNATE SOLUTIONS

1. Ignore the note. It's just a case of infatuation that will eventually go away.

2. Show the note to a colleague whom you can trust and tell him what you know about the situation thus far.

3. Take a serious look at your counseling behavior and your own feelings. In the next counseling session, explain your reaction to the note to D. S.

4. Start counseling with the office door open.

5. Tell D. S. that you care because it is part of your job, and because of who she is, but not to mistake caring and interest for deeper feelings.

6. Call your college professor and ask what others have done in similar situations.

7. Refer D. S. to another counselor.

WHEN JOHNNY GOES MARCHING NORTH

Henry Jourdan, a senior in your school, walks into your office. He's never been in your office before, but you know him to be a well-mannered young man who speaks his piece firmly. You know little about his parents except what you read in the newspaper—the Jourdan name appears often on the society page.

"This is where a student can get help when he's got troubles that he can't talk about to anyone else, right?" asks Henry.

You look at him, wondering how to respond to such a statement. He continues, "Well, I need counseling, or maybe just some information. I don't know. Can you give me some information?"

You answer, "It depends on what type of information you're seeking, but if I don't have it, I'll help you to find it."

"Well, no use beating around the bush. I'll be 18 next week and I don't intend to register for the draft. I want you to give me information on how to get to Canada." What's your approach with Henry?

YOUR SOLUTION

YOUR REACTIONS TO THE ALTERNATE SOLUTIONS

ALTERNATE SOLUTIONS

1. Suggest that his parents probably will understand, and that he should tell them immediately.

2. Tell him to register as a conscientious objector.

3. Help him to realize the consequences of running away to Canada, before you say anything else.

4. Tell him to go ahead and register so that he can graduate. Then if he's drafted, he can resist. The important thing now is to finish high school.

5. Provide him with the information he wants.

UPPERS AND DOWNERS

James Javits, an intelligent senior from a middle-class family has done well in school until this year. You are concerned about the rapid drop in his academic performance and have set up a case conference with all his teachers.

Following a short discussion about James' academic problems, you and the teachers agree that of primary concern are his moods—which range from euphoria to deep depression. Mr. Rankin, his speech teacher, indicates that on certain days James laughs continually for no special reason, while at other times, he seems "spacey." Another teacher said that on some days he's so depressed that he actually causes concern amongst the other students. You and the teachers conclude that James is probably using drugs. It is agreed that you will meet with him for counseling.

You call in James and begin discussing his recent academic problems. He is very depressed and tells you point blank that he has been experimenting with drugs, but that he's not hooked. He realizes that it's affecting his work at school, but it's fun and many times he just can't say "no" because he doesn't want to copout in front of his friends.

You ask James about his extreme moods that occur during the school day, and he indicates that he and some other students have been holding pill parties between classes. James doesn't reveal the names of his friends, and you don't press the issue. You ponder your next move. What will you do?

YOUR SOLUTION

YOUR REACTIONS TO THE ALTERNATE SOLUTIONS

ALTERNATE SOLUTIONS

1. Tell no one about what James has told you, and spend your time helping him to gain the insight and confidence to say no to his friends.

2. Convince James that he should tell you the names of his friends.

3. Your first move should be to inform the school principal and then to check with someone about where you stand legally—regarding the information James gave you about his drug experimentation.

4. Try to convince James that he should discuss this issue with his parents as soon as possible.

5. Try to convince James to turn himself in to the proper authorities.

6. Give James information regarding drug abuse.

THE BLACK-WHITE ENCOUNTER

Your school was one of the last to be racially integrated, and your principal thought your suggestion that some students get together for group discussions was a good idea. Your first group consisted of ten senior volunteers that include both black and whites.

In the first session you indicated that members of the group could say whatever they had on their minds, and it would be an opportunity to get some things out in the open. You hoped that the group would learn new ways of communicating with one another, and would gain a better understanding of themselves.

Yesterday the third session began—again there were negative feelings. Toward the end of the session, Marianne, an attractive black girl, accused Sally, an attractive white girl, of deliberately trying to get the attention of certain black boys. The rest of the blacks laughed at her and this upset one white boy who said, "Don't accuse her because of your low morals." This then angered John, a black, who replied, "I'm tired of you whites always thinking of us as having low morals and crap like that." Things then happened so fast that you weren't sure that you heard all. There were a few threats, but finally the group settled down. You encouraged the group to stop thinking in terms of stereotypes and to cite specific behaviors that produced strong feelings. You wondered about the group ending on an unpleasant note, but at least it was an honest exchange.

This morning the principal called you in and asked, "What in the hell is going on in those groups of yours? I heard that one of yesterday's groups ended up in a fight, knives and all. Is that right? We can't have that going on here. It'll lead either to a riot or at very least some irate parents raising the roof."

You left after explaining a few things about group dynamics and your goals for the group, but he was suspicious and scared. You're meeting with the group again today. What now? What will you do with the group?

YOUR SOLUTION

YOUR REACTIONS TO THE ALTERNATE SOLUTIONS

ALTERNATE SOLUTIONS

1. Tell the group that they are going to have to keep their meetings more confidential because rumors are flying based on half-truths.

2. Structure the group by setting some limits as to topics and ways of expressing ideas and feelings.

3. Get a black co-leader, a teacher or counselor, to help you lead the group.

4. Have the group meet without you.

5. Disband the group until things can cool off and then begin anew.

6. Structure the group so that individuals, and groups of individuals, talk only about the positive things they see in each other. Avoid the negative for now.

7. Focus less on personal matters and discuss matters in general until the group learns to work together.

8. Agree to meet again only if the group agrees not to discuss the meetings outside the group, and only let those who agree remain in the group.

MERLIN THE MAGNIFICENT

One of your counseling colleagues kept the following notes regarding his counseling activities with Merlin Schmidt:

10/5/72   First of the freshman class to be suspended—fighting—two days suspension.

10/8/72   Talked with Merlin about above. Unlike him to fight. He sulks and sneers at me.

10/9/72   Three teachers told me about Merlin. They feel the suspension was too short. All said his work had suddenly gone to pot. Checked his cumulative folder and found that he had excellent marks through eight years. Record also indicates an Otis Quick Scoring IQ of 142.

10/11/72 Called in Merlin to talk. Nothing accomplished.

10/21/72 Ordered psychometric testing for him. WISC verbal score 130, performance 152, full scale 141. Called Mrs. Schmidt to make an appointment for tomorrow.

10/22/72 Merlin's mother has a problem. Her breath almost got me high. Can't work with her. Found out father deserted them around the middle of September.

11/1/72   Merlin sent to me for insubordination. Won't talk to me. Says I'm part of the establishment. Tells me to get off his back.

11/3/72   Noticed Merlin at the ball game sitting with that nice Jones girl. Wonder if they've got something going?

11/8/72   Mid-semester grades came out. Merlin got all F's but one—A in P. E.

11/15/72 Merlin suspended again. Two days for smoking in the restroom. Wonder if military school would be an answer here?

11/21/72 Sent routine letter home to inform mother of Merlin's possible lack of credits to enter 10th grade.

12/1/72   No response from home yet.

12/2/72   Merlin sent to me for swearing in class. Sat and sneered at me again. I'm at my wits' end.

12/3/72   I referred Merlin to another counselor today. Well you can't win 'em all.

OK, you're the other counselor. Your move?

YOUR SOLUTION

YOUR REACTIONS TO THE ALTERNATE SOLUTIONS

ALTERNATE SOLUTIONS

1. Try to work through the Jones girl.
2. Begin to ignore him. Just assign him to detention each time he's sent to you rather than attempting counseling.
3. Call in a social worker.
4. Visit the home and talk to the mother.
5. Call in Merlin.
6. Talk to the P. E. teacher before calling in Merlin.
7. Call for a case conference with all of Merlin's teachers.

DOCTOR, LAWYER, OR INDIAN CHIEF?

Frank Hill, a junior, is the son of a prominent businessman in the community. His father built a small business into a chain of stores, thus the family is financially independent. Frank is a tall, good-looking boy who is one of the school's outstanding athletes. He is popular, but seems more interested in his social life than his academic status. His father is proud of the boy's athletic achievements and expects that Frank will receive an athletic scholarship to the state's major university.

Teachers find Frank likeable, but he is a prankster, and will make remarks in class that are humorous, but also irritating. Teachers complain about his attitude. Some have mixed feelings regarding his being in their class. He generally completes his assignments, but more to get the task done than to learn the subject.

In guidance unit in social studies, Frank listed his career choices in this order: lawyer, doctor, professional athlete. His school records show that he is a C+ student, with A grades in physical education and one business mathematics course. He has received deficiency reports in English and social studies, where he usually struggles between a D and C grade. "A marginal student, at best," said one teacher. Standard achievement scores show: 56 percentile in language usage, 65 percentile in math, and 60 percentile in vocabulary skills. An IQ score of 108, from the fifth grade, is also part of his school records.

When the social studies teacher read his career choices, he stopped by your office and said: "Hey, you'd better counsel that Frank Hill and tell him that he'd better be thinking of something else besides what he put down. He won't even make it to the university, let alone be eligible to play sports. And, he's certainly not big enough to be a professional athlete. He's a dreamer."

You look at the records and ponder what has been said. What's your next move with Frank?

YOUR SOLUTION

YOUR REACTIONS TO THE ALTERNATE SOLUTIONS

ALTERNATE SOLUTIONS

1. Forget Frank and use your time to work with others. Even if he doesn't follow through with his choices, he has an influential family to help him.

2. Call in Frank and ask him to think about himself in terms of his present performance in school, including athletics, and his future career plans.

3. Call in Frank and confront him with the test information you have. Plan a course of action, perhaps a change of classes.

4. Work with Frank indirectly through a small group and present occupational information that will help him think of career fields rather than specific job choices.

5. Call the parents and express your concern as to the incongruence between Frank's career choices and his academic record.

6. Have Frank interview a lawyer, a doctor, and a professional athlete (a little reality testing, perhaps).

NOBODY UNDERSTANDS ME

John is an eleventh-grade student who has met with you before. You think he might regard you as one person at least who tries to understand him. After school one day, he enters your office and talks with you. He says, "I wish I weren't in school. Sometimes it's okay, but most of the time I hate being here . . . . But, it's better than staying home and being nagged. This place . . . they expect so much. Things would be great if I could get away from here—anything is better than this . . . I don't know . . . I might just quit . . . "

You want to respond by saying something helpful and understanding. What's your initial response? (Use a direct quote.)

YOUR SOLUTION

YOUR REACTIONS TO THE ALTERNATE SOLUTIONS

ALTERNATE SOLUTIONS

1. "You're pretty unhappy now and feel things would be easier for you if you weren't in school."

2. "Even though you don't like school, you're still here, and probably because you feel that things would not go well for you if you quit school."

3. "If I understand you, you're saying that you've got a decision to make between staying in school or quitting."

4. "Things are looking bad now, but I'm sure you'll find some way of working things out, and you'll feel better."

5. "What would you do, if you quit school?"

6. "You should talk with the senior counselor about this; he has some interesting information you should know about."

THE PUSHED-OUT

Jimmy is a well-behaved boy from a poor neighborhood. He has some emotional problems and is hampered by an IQ of 80 and a low reading score. You've often spoken with Jimmy and you've wondered how he ever made it to the ninth grade. His teachers have indicated that he's a fine young man, and they feel sorry for him, but he just can't cut the academic subjects. Your school does not have ability grouping, and Jimmy's 80 IQ disqualifies him for special education. He's always on time, tries hard, but continually fails. This morning he wrote you the following note:

> Counsellour—When I go up an down the halls here I no what the teachers are talking about me. They say there goes Jimmy the kid who can't pass nothing. I can't here them but I no, so I walk faster. I thought I would like it here but I doing just like before—gittin all Fs. Sometime mornings are bright till I get here then problems start. I feel left out or like I don't belong here in the first place. I been here now 6 weeks and the teachers don't really no that I don't want to get Fs. I don't mean to say they been mean or anything. But I got F's in everything right now. I am always getting the worst score in all tests in every room. I dunno but I am tired being the dumbest and so today is my last day here and you can bet I'am not comin back no more. You been nice to me so I'am leting you no. Goodby.
>
> Jimmy

What now?

YOUR SOLUTION

YOUR REACTIONS TO THE ALTERNATE SOLUTIONS

ALTERNATE SOLUTIONS

1. Help Jimmy find a job, and encourage him to enroll in the evening vocational school.
2. Try to convince Jimmy to stay in school. Tell him you'll get him a tutor for every subject.
3. Since Jimmy is considered disadvantaged, call a local economic opportunity program and let them handle the situation.
4. Have a case conference with all his teachers and share the note with them.
5. Use this opportunity to talk with the faculty about grading policies and success experiences for low ability students.

THE RUNAWAY

You've been talking with Dorothy Sills, a ninth grader. You know it is difficult for her to get along with her parents. They are very demanding and always disappointed in Dorothy. She is not doing what they expected in school and isn't associating with the "right kind" of friends. Her father once called her "a dirty hippie kid" who will surely end up in trouble. Dorothy has also been grounded on many occasions. Although her father insists that she wear dresses to school, Dorothy uses the school restroom to change into jeans and a baggy shirt. She doesn't want to appear different from her group of friends.

The father talked with you about his disappointment and was genuinely concerned. If Dorothy didn't find new friends and improve in her school work, he threatened to send her to a private school. However, the father really didn't want to separate her from her siblings.

During first period this morning you met with Dorothy, and learned that she had been restricted at home for two weeks. She left the house for a few hours to meet with some friends last night and now her father is furious. Her mother agreed that something had to be done. They decided to take away all extra privileges and set up a strict schedule of activities.

She was adamant about not going home. She didn't know what to do, but wouldn't go home and face the nagging again. You talked about her feelings, what appeared to be alternative ways of working with parents, and how she might improve her school work. But it was obvious that Dorothy was intent on one thing—getting away from it all. She hinted that she might take a bus to another city and stay with a girl friend for awhile.

Dorothy was so depressed that you decided to follow up and see her again later in the day. After third period in the morning Dorothy's name appeared on the absentee list. You learned that her girl friend's name was on the list too. What's your move now?

YOUR SOLUTION

YOUR REACTIONS TO THE ALTERNATE SOLUTIONS

ALTERNATE SOLUTIONS

1. Call her parents and notify them that Dorothy has left school and that she may be running away.

2. Notify the police that the girls are missing and are probable runaways.

3. Call the home to see if Dorothy went home sick.

4. Leave school yourself and see if you can find her, perhaps starting down at the bus depot.

5. Notify the principal of what you know, and let him handle it from there.

6. Call in a few of Dorothy's friends and ask them what they know about the matter. Get as much information as you can before making a decision to notify others.

7. Do nothing. Dorothy might need your help later as a counselor and friend. Any other action might jeopardize the relationship.

8. Dorothy was obviously asking you to stop her from running away. Get as many people as you can involved in doing just that.

THE COUNSELOR AS A COUNSELOR

During the past decade the work of the counselor has become a recognized part of most secondary schools in our nation. Over the years there has been a steady increase in the number of counselors, as well as literature supporting the integration of the counseling function into the total school program. Although the position of school counselor has finally reached a stage where it is considered a normal part of the educational system, there is still some misunderstanding and confusion as to the role and function of the counselor.

Some of the confusion is because of the lack of clarity regarding the major functions and responsibilities of the counselor. A general description of a counselor's role may not fit exactly you and your school system, but it might be helpful in clarifying what could and should be expected.

As a counselor you will work as a human behavior and relationship specialist. Two years of graduate study in counselor education, with an emphasis in psychology and human development, will prove beneficial when working in a helping relationship. There are four major functions that counselors tend to perform: (1) counseling students, (2) consulting with teachers, administrators, and parents regarding students, (3) studying and analyzing student populations, and interpreting results for other educators, and (4) coordinating mental health and vocational resources within the school and between the school and community. All counselors, of course, are limited in their ability to perform activities related to these functions by their own competency and the particular realities of a school setting. However, any activity that is not related to one of these four functions should not be expected or encouraged as a part of a counselor's job.

What is counseling? Counseling is defined as a personal and dynamic relationship between a professionally prepared counselor and an individual (or a group of individuals), where the purpose is to assist that individual in his understanding of himself and his environment. This special learning process usually involves the exploration of feelings and behaviors as they are related to decision-making processes that affect personal growth and development. The counseling process many times leads a student to identify alternate solutions to his problems and to plan a positive course of action.

Unfortunately, there also remains a great deal of confusion as to the difference between the terms guidance and counseling. Guidance has been defined by some as any activity that enables an individual student to express himself and to enhance his potential within the context of the school setting. This definition is too general and creates the problem of establishing an identity for guidance that is independent of teaching and administrative functions. Although both teachers and administrators will be involved in a guidance program, guidance is significantly different from both teaching and administration. Guidance can best be defined as a broad spectrum of activities that focuses on the management of human relations within a school setting so that each student's unique characteristics can be enhanced.

As a counselor you might be involved in some school guidance activities that can be independent of counseling. For example, you will be expected to provide students with information and advice regarding vocational and educational plans. Most likely you will be the person to see when a schedule of classes needs to be arranged or changed. Among your other guidance activities may be: planning homeroom guidance programs, directing the testing program, working with the student council, planning guidance-oriented school assembly programs, and having the responsibility for the cumulative folders.

Because of a possible misunderstanding regarding your role you may be involved in activities that are not even remotely related to either guidance or counseling. For example, you may feel a great deal of pressure to take attendance, patrol the halls, monitor the lunchroom, do substitute teaching, score test materials, or perhaps even administer some form of punishment to a student. To some administrators, you will be just another assistant who can help in minor jobs around the school. To some teachers you will be viewed as a specialist who is on the periphery of the real action. They might wonder how what you do affects their work.

As a professionally trained guidance counselor you will want to give high priority to counseling students, both individually and in groups. You will want to use your time in those guidance activities that uniquely contribute to the education of students. At one point in the history of education, counseling and guidance in the schools tended to focus on vocational information and planning. Later, educational adjustment and planning were included. In some cases, counselors were discouraged from working with emotional and social problems because these problems were not seen as part of the school's responsibility. It is now widely accepted that education means working with the whole child, not just a few aspects of him. His problems lie in more than just vocational and educational areas. When he attends school, he brings all of his problems with him, which affects his learning. Now, more than at any other time, as a counselor and educator you will be asked to take more responsibility for the development of the total person, and to assume an active part in the emotional and social growth of students.

How far does the school go in its concern for the whole child? What services should the school provide in attempting to remedy the psychological problems of students? Should a school counselor practice psychotherapy, although time and cost prohibit the traditional practice of psychotherapy in the school? Most likely, psychotherapy will be provided by outside agencies and institutions. The school is concerned with mental health, but it is not a health clinic.

Counseling and psychotherapy share more common elements than differences, but a distinction does exist. Most simply defined, psychotherapy implies a deep involvement on both the part of the therapist and the patient, and it is generally concerned with personality reorganization. Also, patients in psychotherapy generally exhibit extreme modes of maladjustment. Counseling tends to be concerned more with present, conscious material, while psychotherapeutic approaches are more apt to deal with historic and symbolic materials in the patient's unconscious. You will work with all kinds of student problems. Rather than focusing on deep-seated conflicts, or reconstructing the whole personality, you will probably direct your efforts toward minimum changes. As the student experiences this educative or reeducative counseling process, he will move in the direction of being a fully functioning individual.

As a counselor you will be familiar with several counseling theories. In your training you will have experimented with various approaches and techniques. You will no doubt want to follow a sound rationale of human behavior and attempt to apply scientific methods in your work. Counseling is not something to be taken lightly. To simply talk to a student doesn't necessarily make a difference. Rather, you will want to talk *with* the person *not at him.* You will want to know what the student is thinking, recognizing that change often begins when thoughts are verbalized, even if they are not fully understood. Consequently, your knowledge of counseling theory and approaches alone probably will not make a significant difference. Counseling begins and ends with the focus on the helping relationship.

What will determine whether or not a student will talk with you about himself? Under what conditons will he disclose those matters that are of a personal concern to him? In your counseling relationship, what must the student experience before he can wholeheartedly commit himself to self-examination and change?

THE ART AND SCIENCE OF LISTENING

Regardless of age, everyone appreciates a good listener—an essential aspect of effective counseling. In order to be a good listener, one must avoid being preoccupied with his own feelings and ideas, or overly absorbed with the daily routine. A counselor listens attentively, but listening is more than just hearing words. Listening involves looking at the person and being with him as he expresses himself through gestures, tone of voice, and unique expressions. Effective listening is using a third ear and eye.

For many students you will be a significant person in their lives, simply because of your ability to listen and to care. Our society has produced a population of talkers—people who like to talk about everything. When an individual engages in conversation he rarely finds people who respond so as to give him an opportunity to continue talking about the idea he has introduced. Rather, most people tend to wait their turn to speak, and then relate an incident in their own lives which seems to be relevant. If you are to be an effective counselor, you will want to focus your attention and comments on the student's interests and needs and not on your own. In general, your commitment to listening and really hearing what the student is saying is directly related to your ability to genuinely care.

THE CORE DIMENSIONS OF THE COUNSELING RELATIONSHIPS

Within the last decade we have learned through research a great deal about counseling and psychotherapy. One of the most important insights this research gives us is that there are a few facilitative dimensions or conditions that are a necessary part of all effective counseling relationships. Among these are respect, empathy, and genuineness.

Respect. When a counselor respects a student he communicates a positive regard for him. Such terms as "unconditional positive regard" and "nonpossessive warmth" have been used to describe that which an individual experiences when he feels valued for his personal worth as a free individual. A high regard for the student emphasizes that his personal dignity is valued, his personal feelings are accepted, and that he is not judged. The degree to which you can communicate your respect to a student will eventually define the area of a person's life that can be freely explored.

Some students have low self-regard which is due in part to experiences where their feelings and behaviors were not accepted or valued. As these students begin to experience your respect for them, they will stop defending themselves long enough to seriously examine their patterns of living. Your respect can break down the barriers of isolation and pave the way for close communication and new self-esteem.

Empathy. Empathy means understanding another person, especially what he is feeling. It involves going beyond the mere expression of words and intellectual ideas to a deeper level of understanding. You have probably heard the expression "put yourself in the other person's shoes," but this does not mean you must be that other person. When you have empathy for a student, you will have an awareness of his internal frame of reference. At times this will entail abandoning the lofty position of an all-knowing adult and educator to experience the student's feelings. Identifying for a moment can help, although you will never wholly understand another individual.

In your efforts to be perceived as an understanding person, you may find it helpful to precede any advice, information, praise, or support with comments which imply that you are attempting to understand the student's world. Your attempts to perceive and verbalize the student's feelings tell him more than anything else that you are trying to understand him, regardless of whether your statements are accurate or not. It puts a "chip in the bank" toward the development of a nonthreatening, facilitative, counselor-student relationship. A few "chip in the bank" statements can help create that subjective bond which is needed for effective counseling.

Certainly there is more to counseling than a relationship. however, if the facilitative relationship is not present, you will find your students pulling back into their proverbial shells—much as tortoises do defensively—

and your words will never be integrated into their perceptual fields. There will be times when you will want to offer advice, information, or directions, but you will first want to make sure that the student is "out of the shell." As a student experiences a relatively nonthreatening counseling relationship, which includes the dimensions of respect and empathy, he is much more apt to consider the alternative suggestions and methods you may offer to help him to change his behavior.

The mode of communicating empathic understanding is often a topic of controversy within professional circles. Is the ability to empathize a special talent reserved for a few sensitive people, or can it be taught? There is considerable evidence that empathic understanding is not a characteristic of the general population and is often lacking in many people who are employed in helping professions. Apparently tuning in on a student's wave length can be an acquired skill, but it does take much practice. Once you have grasped part of what the student is experiencing and feeling, it is important that you somehow communicate this to him.

Genuineness. "Telling it like it is" has become a popular expression among the younger generation. Students are suspicious of adults who talk one way and live another. They deplore hypocrisy. To them it is a time for truth, loving, and communicating; but, it must all be honest.

Being genuine implies not playing a role. It means being in tune with yourself and acting in a way that reveals congruence with students. If a counselor experiences conflict, and is inconsistent in what he is feeling and how he is acting, the stage is set for him to be perceived as a phony. It is very difficult to feel one thing and to communicate the opposite.

Genuineness may be the most important characteristic of any helping relationship, although it is limiting by itself. It can sometimes make unknowing helpers out of persons in your school simply because students can depend on them for an honest response. Some counselors, even though they have studied under the best instructors, and have participated in sensitivity training, and learned systematic ways of responding, still play at being counselors. When they assume some kind of therapeutic role that is not characteristic of themselves, their ability to positively facilitate others will decline, and they may not be helpful at all. If you are to be an effective counselor, you will want to functionally integrate counseling theory and essential helping behaviors into your personality.

There are other dimensions of a counseling relationship which could be mentioned. They have been variously described as self-disclosure, spontaneity, warmth, caring, openness, concreteness, flexibility, intensity, sensitivity, and humor. However, none has proved to be more essential than those mentioned above. Eventually the characteristics combine into what might be known as "the good guy syndrome." When a student comes into contact with a counselor he can call "a good guy" he is saying that here is a person with whom I can risk a part of myself, someone to whom I can open up and be vulnerable because he cares about me.

You will no doubt come into contact with many professional educators, including some counselors, who will not seem very effective. Despite all their good intentions they are simply incapable of creating or expressing the facilitative dimensions. There was a time when we considered them not very effective, or hoped that they had no ill effect on students. Unfortunately, recent studies indicate that counseling can be for better or for worse. That is to say, without the essential facilitative conditions as ingredients in the counseling relationship, it is possible that the counselor's work can have a detrimental effect on students. Some research has shown that students not only fail to attain their goals in counseling, but actually become worse, if they do not experience these primary dimensions.

There are some students who are so deprived of positive relationships that your meeting with them alone will enhance their development. For others, you will want to use more active approaches including modeling, behavior modification, behavioral contracts, reality testing, skill training, and disseminating information. Regardless of your approach or technique, the relationship is essential.

As you become effective in your work, you are going to become exposed to a wide range of students and problems. Your behavior will speak for itself, and it will not be necessary to tell students that counselors keep things in confidence in order to gain their trust, they will sense it, and know it through their experience with you.

In years past, counseling was always considered as part of a crisis situation. Supposedly, students sought out a counselor when they were experiencing difficulties and didn't know with whom else to talk. It is now recognized that counselors can be more effective when they meet with students before a crisis occurs. This means that you will be involved in identifying students with whom to work. For example, you will meet with students individually and in groups to help them expand self-awareness and become acquainted with ways in which to approach problem solving situations.

Finally, if you are to be an effective counselor you must take a serious look at yourself. It is time to face the truth and examine your own hang ups. Increasing your own self-understanding will give you the freedom to work with the problems of others. Everyone has their own biases and prejudices which no doubt creep into the counseling relationship. At times your own personal values will be exposed; however, it is important that these be tempered and restrained to the point that they are not imposed on your counselees. Learning counseling theories, approaches, and techniques, and studying yourself and others are valuable in helping you become a successful counselor. But as you enter your first counseling position, it might best be remembered that what helps most is a genuine interest in listening and talking with kids.

FOR FURTHER READING

Glasser, W. *Reality Therapy*. New York: Harper and Row Publishers, 1965.

Krumboltz, J. D., and Thoresen, C. E. *Behavioral Counseling: Cases and Techniques*. New York: Holt, Rinehart and Winston, 1969.

Lewis, E. C. *The Psychology of Counseling*. New York: Holt, Rinehart and Winston, 1970.

Mahler, C. *Group Counseling In The Schools*. Boston: Houghton Mifflin Co., 1969.

Ohlsen, M. *Group Counseling*. New York: Holt, Rinehart and Winston, 1970.

Patterson, C. H. *Counseling and Psychotherapy: Theory and Practice*. New York: Harper and Row Publishers, 1966.

Rogers, C. *On Becoming A Person*. Boston: Houghton Mifflin Co., 1961.

Stefflre, B. *Theories of Counseling*. New York: McGraw-Hill Book Co., 1965.

CHAPTER TWO

The Counselor as a Consultant

PYGMALION IN THE CLASSROOM

Mrs. Campbell is a difficult teacher to work with to say the least. Each year the story is the same. She tells you that such and such a person just won't do well and should be transferred out of her advanced math class before it is too late. More often that not, she's right when it comes to identifying students who will do poorly.

This day in the teachers' lounge Mrs. Campbell calls you over and asks you to look at Bill Daley's class record. She says, "I'm concerned about this boy. I told you earlier that he just shouldn't have been placed in the class. He's going to have a lot of trouble keeping up, and I'll have to send out a deficiency report each grading period." Looking over her shoulder, you see a sporadic pattern of grades and think to yourself that Bill isn't very consistent. Then you notice that beside each name is a figure. It didn't make sense until Mrs. Campbell said, "Bill just doesn't have as high an IQ as some of his friends, and it makes it impossible for him to do well." You now realize that Mrs. Campbell has been to the school files and recorded each student's IQ score beside the name in her grade book. You know Bill Daley personally and think he's an intelligent boy. He does well in all his other classes. If anything, you seriously doubt the validity of the recorded score which suggests average intelligence (IQ = 105).

As Mrs. Campbell walks off to class she turns to say, "Well, we can wait and see, but I can tell you now that he probably won't make it." Knowing Mrs. Campbell, he probably won't. What do you do?

YOUR SOLUTION

YOUR REACTIONS TO THE ALTERNATE SOLUTIONS

ALTERNATE SOLUTIONS

1. Set up an appointment with Mrs. Campbell and explain that one should speak of IQ scores, not IQ; and, this is only one sample of a boy's ability.

2. Provide Mrs. Campbell with some information on test interpretation, with particular emphasis upon the use and limitations of tests.

3. Drop by her room and show her how Bill's IQ score could range between 115 and 95, based on the standard error of measurement. Suggest that Bill is more likely in the higher range.

4. Call in Bill and give him another test. If he scores higher, give the information to Mrs. Campbell.

5. Confront Mrs. Campbell by telling her that it appears as if she is using IQ scores as a guide to labeling students, and that this can become a dangerous self-fulfilling prophecy.

6. Approach the problem indirectly. Have a meeting with all teachers on the faculty, and talk to them about the interpretation and use of intelligence tests.

FATHER KNOWS BEST

The first week in March, Mr. and Mrs. Wells make an appointment to talk with you about the rapid decline in their son's grades. Randy (WISC of 142) is an immature 12-year-old eighth grader. His grades have averaged around the C level for the past two years. His cumulative record includes straight A's up through the sixth grade. His record also indicates he was double promoted in the third grade.

Randy's parents tell you of their concern regarding his social immaturity. Many of his friends are still in elementary school. Finally, Mrs. Wells comes to the point. They want Randy held over in the eighth grade rather than promoted. You ask them if they have talked to Randy about this. They indicate that they have and he is opposed. Mr. Wells makes it clear that regardless of Randy's feelings they want him held back for his own good. As the Wells' leave your office, they make it clear that they feel that it's your job to convince Randy that this is best for him.

Randy is called in. He tells you that he's been losing a lot of sleep worrying about his being held back. He states that his grades are good enough to get into the ninth grade, the last year in junior high, and that everyone will laugh at him if he is held back. As he leaves your office he bluntly states: "I won't be held back."

Today his parents are coming in again to see you. What are you going to tell them?

YOUR SOLUTION

YOUR REACTIONS TO THE ALTERNATE SOLUTIONS

ALTERNATE SOLUTIONS

1. Tell them that there is no reason to retain Randy in the eighth grade.

2. Suggest that Randy spend two years in the ninth grade. In this way his classmates will move over to the high school and there will be less taunting.

3. Pull out the research that shows that many children with exceptional intelligence have social problems and that it's perfectly normal for a bright eighth grader to be playing with elementary school children.

4. Call Randy into the conference with the intention of arriving at a compromise solution.

5. Tell the parents that it's Randy's life and that it should be his decision.

I'VE HAD IT!

Bill Weatherford was a history major in college and graduated with honors. He was eager to begin his first year of teaching and you were glad to see him join the faculty as a world history teacher. He is energetic, verbally skilled, and seemed like the kind of young man who would get along well with students. He certainly knew his subject matter.

Before long, however, it was apparent that Bill was having difficulty with students in his classes. Some labeled his class a real drag. Bill was beginning to agree with them. He responded by working longer hours at night preparing his lectures, reviewing his college notes, and looking through his books to find little incidents in history that might stimulate the class. He tried telling jokes, but this too met with mixed reactions and students were becoming more restless each day. Last week Bill became angry with two students for not paying attention and sent someone out of class for the first time this year.

On this occasion, Bill entered your office and said, "Hey, I've got a couple of guys in my history class who are really driving me crazy—Bill Adams and Kerry Stone. They don't care about learning anything, at least not from me. They upset the whole class. How about getting them transferred to someone else?"

It was obvious that Bill wanted to talk some more and about other things. He pulled up a chair, sat down, and continued: "Wow, what a day! You know it's days like these that make me want to throw in the towel and go back to graduate school full time. I think I'd like teaching in college." He looks at you, shakes his head a little, and shrugs his shoulders. What does Bill want from you? What do you do?

YOUR SOLUTION

YOUR REACTIONS TO THE ALTERNATE SOLUTIONS

ALTERNATE SOLUTIONS

1. Bill needs support. Suggest that all teachers have their good and bad days. Perhaps say, "Don't worry Bill, you'll get the feel of it as you get more experience."

2. Bill needs counseling. Focus on his interest in college teaching. He is ambivalent about where he thinks he can best work and he's questioning his ability to teach high school students.

3. Bill needs consulting. Listen to his feelings about teaching and then focus on his relationship with his students. Help him examine his teaching methods in terms of how students feel about the class.

4. Bill needs advice. Advise him to quit lecturing and start putting himself in the students' shoes.

5. Bill needs help in discipline. Tell him that you'll talk with the boys and see if you can get them to be more cooperative in class. If that doesn't work, then perhaps a transfer would be best.

6. Bill needs more knowledge about students. Get out the records of the two boys and see what you can do to help Bill work with them.

7. Bill needs an evaluation of his teaching.

THE MEDDLER

At the beginning of the school year an in-service speaker encouraged the teachers in your school to seek greater understanding of students. He emphasized that many times teachers are unaware of the unique problems and life styles of students. Consequently, teachers often fail in their attempts to individualize instruction and meet the needs of a child.

One of the school's teachers, Mrs. Keene, thought it was a good idea to examine the school records in an attempt to become more familiar with her students. You went over some with her. However, information was sparse and completely missing in some cases. Mrs. Keene decided to administer some standardized tests which might give her an idea of her students' self-concepts. In addition, she developed a questionnaire that allowed them to describe relationships with others, most pressing problems, most happy and sad times, and a few other items. She hoped that this information would provide the insight and understanding that would enable her to work more effectively with each student.

Today you have an appointment with Mr. and Mrs. Jack Brunner. Their daughter, Jeanne, is in Mrs. Keene's class. You didn't know that was important until they arrived. They came straight to the point. It concerned them that Mrs. Keene was prying into matters that were "none of her business." They resented anyone snooping into their daughter's personal life and felt it was Mrs. Keene's job to teach social studies and not meddle with the private lives of children and their families.

They look at you. What now?

YOUR SOLUTION

YOUR REACTIONS TO THE ALTERNATE SOLUTIONS

ALTERNATE SOLUTIONS

1. Assure the Brunners that the tests and questionnaires were given with the best of intentions and present a rationale by summarizing the in-service speaker's remarks.

2. Call in Mrs. Keene and let her handle it.

3. Tell the Brunners that you will get Jeanne's tests and questionnaires from Mrs. Keene and destroy them.

4. Agree that this is probably an unwarranted invasion of privacy and say that you will take what steps you can to see that it doesn't happen again.

5. Encourage the Brunners to let Jeanne make the decision as to whether she wants Mrs. Keene to have the information. It's optional and it's her private life.

6. Thank the Brunners for coming and stall until you can discuss the issue with the faculty and principal.

CARRY A BIG STICK

Mr. Hummel is principal of Jackson High School. He believes that every good school is founded on firm discipline. According to him, without discipline, learning cannot take place. He's active in enforcing school policies, most of which he has made. Teachers have been reprimanded by him for "letting kids get away with too much." Some teachers are threatened and feel that they can't be themselves in the classroom. Others say that it is essential to have a tough principal on the job in order to handle the problem students.

As the school's counselor, you remember when a few older girls brought their alumni boy friends to an after-game dance. When it was learned later that some of them had been smoking marijuana, Mr. Hummel promptly announced at a school assembly that there would be no more after-game dances. Students moaned and complained that it wasn't fair to punish all for the actions of a few. Hummel replied that if they had been concerned about their social activities they would have been more responsible and not allowed such inappropriate behavior to occur.

Since Mr. Hummel became principal three years ago there seems to have been an increase in writing on the walls, gouges in the woodwork, broken windows, and tire marks on the school lawn. These behaviors appear to be an expression of defiance to authority. Hummel remarks that without his tough policies things would be even worse.

Four of the best teachers approach you and ask for a conference. They tell you that some teachers are thinking of leaving because of the school's stiffling atmosphere. One of them says, "The learning climate in the school is so miserable that even our best students are being affected by it. Many of the top kids have joined the hoods in a common cause—fight the establishment. They talk about it constantly and a day never goes by when they are not complaining about school. This kind of discussion takes precedence over academic interests. There is an unrest at the school that makes it unpleasant to be a part of the faculty." You listen and agree that something needs to be done. At the end of the conference the teachers ask you to consult with Mr. Hummel and put him straight on matters.

You want to help, but how?

YOUR SOLUTION

YOUR REACTIONS TO THE ALTERNATE SOLUTIONS

ALTERNATE SOLUTIONS

1. Tell the teachers that they have the power base and that they should organize and present their grievances to the principal as a united faculty.

2. Tell the teachers that you would be willing to work with them on a grievance committee, but that all of the members should meet with Mr. Hummel and express their concerns.

3. Send out a questionnaire to the faculty and find out their satisfactions as well as complaints.

4. Work through the student council and serve primarily as a mediator and facilitator of communication between students, teacher, and principal.

5. Meet with Mr. Hummel in private and try to convince him that some of his methods have caused unrest.

6. Work through the superintendent's office and ask for help.

THE MEDIATOR

One of your duties in the guidance office is to help students plan their schedule of classes and to place them in certain sections. In doing this, you consider plans upon graduation, current achievement, and recommendations from teachers.

Dale Rogers, is an average sophomore who is enrolled in college preparatory classes, but not the advanced ones. He is active in many school activities and is well-liked, but he has trouble studying and receives grades that suggest he will have academic problems in college.

Although Dale made a C- grade in geometry, he was not recommended for advanced math classes. In addition, he was not recommended for second year French because his teacher felt that he would be unable to keep up and would most likely receive failing grades.

After talking with Dale you learned that he isn't interested in French. However, despite his marginal grades in geometry, he wants to take more math because it fits his plans of someday becoming an engineer. He expects to study more next year and thinks he will probably do better under a different teacher.

Mr. and Mrs. Rogers would not sign the course approval form, which did not include advanced math or French. They wanted to talk with you. During a conference it was clear that Dale's parents expected him to enter a certain college that required two years of a foreign language. Moreover, they thought Dale should take more math because it was needed in many career fields and it seemed foolish to stop taking math at the end of his sophomore year. "He has a right to take those classes because they are offered and we are taxpayers who support this school for our children. It's also not fair for teachers to prejudge Dale. With extra study this summer, we know that he can keep up." You know that both teachers base their recommendations upon past experience. What do you do?

YOUR SOLUTION

YOUR REACTIONS TO THE ALTERNATE SOLUTIONS

ALTERNATE SOLUTIONS

1. Tell the parents that the teachers are the best judge of Dale's academic record and that he will not be able to take the courses suggested by the parents.

2. Tell the teachers that the parents are making this special request and let the teachers make the final decision as to placement.

3. Tell the parents and teachers that the decision should be Dale's.

4. Call for a conference with all parties present, including Dale, and see if a compromise can be reached.

5. Suggest enrollment on a trial basis. At the end of six weeks let his record determine whether he should continue or not.

6. Enroll him in summer school and get a tutor for next year. If these conditions are met, let him take the advanced classes.

HEY, GOT A MINUTE?

You're having lunch with a counseling colleague from another school. Discussion focuses on general school news. Finally, he says, "Hey, let me ask you something. What would you do if someone on your faculty asked for counseling? I mean, there's a teacher in our school who first came to see me because of some problems that she was having with a few students. We talked together and then at the end of our conference she mentioned that things weren't going well at home either. She said she was having some marital problems, but didn't elaborate. She just asked if I'd help by counseling with her. I really didn't know what to do or say, so I said we'd talk about it later. What do you think I should do?" How will you react to your counselor friend's request?

YOUR SOLUTION

YOUR REACTIONS TO THE ALTERNATE SOLUTIONS

ALTERNATE SOLUTIONS

1. Suggest that he explore referral agencies with her and not counsel her.
2. Meet with her for counseling if it will affect her work in the classroom.
3. Indicate that professional ethics prevent him from counseling her on personal matters.
4. Suggest that he focus primarily on teacher-student relationships and only incidentally on marital problems.
5. Respond to the counselor's concern and feelings, but don't give advice.

THE COUNSELOR AS A CONSULTANT

The counseling literature implies that from two-thirds to three-fourths of a counselor's time should be committed to the functions of (1) counseling students and (2) consulting with teachers, administrators, and parents, as they in turn work with students. Although counseling has been researched and described in the professional literature for many years, this has not been true of consultation. While consultation may have been practiced, counselors have only recently given it careful attention. Consultation is important because of the realistic limitation that a counselor faces in attempting to meet the guidance and counseling needs of all students.

The American School Counselor Association has recommended a ratio of one full-time qualified counselor to each 250-300 high school students. It is assumed that such a ratio would enable most counselors to become fully acquainted with their counselees and provide adequate counseling services. However, even this recommended ratio will not allow the counselor to adequately meet all student needs.

In many schools the guidance and counseling program is geared to practices that were appropriate for other times and other conditions. For example, it is clear to anyone who has worked in schools that the traditional method of "trouble shooting"—working with each crisis as it arises—is not appropriate for today. Unfortunately, in actual practice this is the major emphasis in most schools, since it is the student in trouble who is likely to receive the most attention from his teachers and other specialized personnel. The students who create disturbances in class, who are in trouble academically, who are habitually truant, or who are unable to get along with others, are the ones most likely to be recommended to you for counseling. Operating a "repair business" is a necessary part of counseling. Most counselors dislike it because it does not produce the greatest returns for time and effort expended. Problems which have been building up for a long time rarely respond to quick treatment. When a student is experiencing an intense crisis, he tends to guard himself against others and to become defensive of his position. At best, you will seek and obtain minimum gains in crisis situations.

Effective guidance programs are founded on a developmental, rather than a remedial base. When a program has a developmental orientation there is a focus on the emotional and educational requirements of all children. The major rationale for consultation with teachers stems from the belief that guidance objectives can only be obtained for all students through work with all teachers.

The counselor-student ratio in most schools will limit counseling and force guidance programs to emphasize a remedial approach, unless consultation is given high priority. As a teacher develops new insights about students, he increases his ability to become more proficient in aiding the growth of students, and thus reduces the number that need to be seen by a specialist, such as a counselor. Studies of student-teacher relationships indicate that those teachers who know the most about their students and who are sensitive to their needs and interests tend to have more influence on a greater number of students than teachers whose most important focus is knowledge of subject matter. There is no doubt that teachers differ a great deal in the amount of information they have about students and the way in which they use this information. It will be your job to help teachers use information wisely and productively.

There is little doubt that a teacher's understanding of a student's behavior can enhance teaching effectiveness. Research with children has been done where they were matched according to age, intelligence, achievement, and home background. When teachers were given help with information on each child, it seems that they had a much more positive effect upon students, as exhibited by fewer psychological conflicts and disturbances, greater academic progress, and a positive attitude toward school, as compared to cases where teachers were not given assistance. There is also some evidence to indicate that working with a student directly through teacher consultation may well be as effective as counseling directly with the student.

Although the art of communication is the common ingredient in both counseling and consultation, these two processes must be clearly differentiated if you are to be effective as both a counselor and a consultant.

Almost all authorities agree that the basic interpersonal dimensions of empathy, regard, respect, warmth, genuineness, openness, etc. are essential in forming a helping relationship. Consultation definitely requires these basic core dimensions. However, in consultation, the teacher does not seek the depth of self-understanding that he would through counseling. This is because the consultant focuses on some unit, such as a student, instructional method, or course content that is external to the consultee or teacher. This is not to say that feelings, conflicts, or the need system of an individual are avoided entirely or ignored. Rather, consultation does not provide the kind of setting for an extensive investment in exploration of self-dynamics. Most often teachers seek your help when they are having trouble with a particular student. At that time they are feeling inadequate and in need of outside help. Since consultation is not concerned with personality reorganization of the teacher, the question becomes: what can you do for the teacher? The answer certainly is more than a simple communication of empathy and the other core interpersonal dimensions of a helping relationship. Several guidelines have proven helpful in consultation and are discussed.

BE A LISTENER

Regardless of the problem presented, the consultee needs to talk out his feelings and ideas about the troublesome situation. As the teacher is talking, you will want to be an attentive listener and encourage the teacher to bare his feelings. In this respect, the first step of consultation represents a catharsis for the teacher. It is needed if a more rational approach to the problem is to be developed. The more the teacher talks in the beginning, the more there is a tendency to reduce anxiety and create an atmosphere for rational thinking. The more intense the crisis, the more important it is to help the teacher to vent his feelings.

BE A SELECTIVE LISTENER

An analysis of any conversation between most people indicates that talk is rapid and several ideas are introduced. Ideas are not necessarily put together in logical sequence or order. As a consultant you will not be able to absorb or respond to everything that the teacher reports. Therefore, it is important that you be a selective listener. That is to say, you should listen for (1) feelings of the teacher, (2) specific behaviors which have led the teacher to make certain inferences about the student, (3) what the teacher seems to expect in the situation, (4) what he has done up to this time, and (5) positive attitudes and behaviors that are already present.

BE A SELECTIVE RESPONDER

Many times counselors forget that the same communication responses that work in counseling are often effective in other kinds of conversations. As a consultant you will want to call upon your best communicative skills when talking with teachers about their students. Be selective in the kinds of responses that you make in order that you can bring about a more systematic approach to resolving the problem.

In general, it is best to avoid rushing in with advice or recipes for change. Teachers are somewhat suspicious of specialists and they have often said, "Their advice never seems to work." Other statements that are frequently made include, "They don't understand the situation"; "They have some great ideas, but they aren't very practical"; "Their ideas are difficult to put into practice when you are working with 35 students." As a general rule, people tend to resist advice and usually respond to it with something like "Yes, but . . . . " or "I agree, however . . . . " That is to say people who receive quick advice tend to defend themselves, present other points of view, or tell why the advice is inappropriate.

In addition to avoiding giving advice too soon, proceed cautiously with interpretating behavior. Unless you feel it is going to benefit the teacher's immediate overall perception of the student, or help the teacher to modify the student's behavior in the immediate future, interpretations are best offered at a later time when it is part of a rationale for a plan of action. Interpretations, like advice, often meet with resistance when they are presented too early. Teachers complain about counselors who meet with them in consultation and give them a textbook diagnosis which doesn't seem to be very helpful. For example, "John has a poor self-concept and needs special attention"; "Barbara has parents who are divorced and that is one of the reasons why she needs so much extra teacher attention"; or "Bob has a problem accepting authority figures and this is one of the reasons why he argues back in class."

As a consultant instead of premature advice or classical interpretation, you may first want to reflect the feelings of the teacher so that he will continue to talk and present all aspects of the problem. Responses such as, "Bill has really upset you today"; "You're feeling frustrated after having tried so many things"; or "I can see how concerned you are for him," tend to communicate respect, regard, and empathy, which is most likely what the teacher needs in the beginning of consultation.

After the teacher has talked about some of his own feelings you will want to help him to focus on the specific behaviors which have led to the concerns about the student. It is your job to clarify the behaviors which have led to the problem, especially if the teacher says, "This boy is really disturbed and needs help," or "She is so lazy and tends to just cause trouble in the classroom." It is important to know what behaviors have led the teacher to conclude that he is lazy, in trouble all the time, or emotionally disturbed. The behaviors not only serve as a measure of the need for change, but can be useful criteria in establishing goals and measuring results.

As the teacher is talking you will want to listen for and acknowledge the behaviors, the positive feelings, and attitudes, which the teacher has wards the student. Most teachers need some reassurance that they have been doing something right to help the student and have not been totally inadequate. Statements like "You know, I can tell that you were really irritated at that time, but you were able to keep from embarrassing him in front of the class and this probably avoided making him become defensive"; or, "Although you feel he is uncooperative, you like him because he can be stimulating in a conversation," keep the focus on the positive, which is necessary at times before other approaches can be considered.

BE A RESOURCE PERSON

Your training has prepared you as an expert in human behavior and interpersonal relationships. However, on many occasions you will need to review the professional literature regarding a particular problem under attentions. You will want to collect research studies, authoritative opinions, and appropriate reading materials for the teacher and yourself. This material can be helpful in providing a rationale for a plan of action and will perhaps suggest procedures that could bring about a change in student's behavior.

BE A TEAM MEMBER

As a consultant you become an active part of an education team Together, you and the teacher can identify specific behaviors that are to be elicited or extinguished, or patterns of behaviors which would suggest change in self-concept or attitude. Together, you will want to consider hypotheses which lead to alternate plans of action. After all alternatives are considered, you and the teacher will together plan a systematic course of action. On too many occasions teachers leave a counselor's office with nebulous thoughts instead of specific recommendations and guidelines that are supported by a psychological rationale, research evidence, and careful thinking. Although the ultimate responsibility for carrying out a plan of action or making decisions in the classroom lies with the teacher, teachers respect counselors who work closely with them.

The above discussion has been almost entirely aimed at consultation with teachers; and, as a school counselor most of your consultation will be with teachers. However, you will find yourself consulting with administrators, parents, counselor colleagues, and others as they work with students. In general, the consultation procedures discussed above will apply to most any type of consultee. You will not want to give up your counseling activities in order to increase consultation opportunities. Perhaps the ideal role today would be to become a counselor-consultant.

FOR FURTHER READING

Caplain, G. *Mental Health and Consultation.* Chapter 8, U. S. Department of H.E.W.: Childrens Bureau, 1959.

Dinkmeyer, D. C. "The Counselor as Consultant to the Teacher." *School Counselor* 14 (1967): 294-97.

Dinkmeyer, D. C. and Caldwell, C. E. *Developmental Counseling and Guidance.* Chapters 9 and 10. New York: McGraw-Hill Book Co., 1970.

Faust, V. *The Counselor-Consultant in the Elementary School* Chapters 2, 3, and 4. Boston: Houghton Mifflin Co., 1968

Fullmer, D. "Family Group Consultation." In *Theories and Methods of Group Counseling in the School,* edited by George Gazda 181-207. Springfield, Ill.: Charles C Thomas, 1969.

Lundquist, G. W., and Chamley, J. C. "Counselor-Consultant: A Move Toward Effectiveness." *School Counselor* 18 (1971): 362-66.

Newman, R. G. *Psychological Consultation in the Schools.* New York: Basic Books, 1967.

Wittmer, J. "The School Counselor: A Catalyst in the Guidance Program." *School Counselor* 18 (1971): 342-48.

CHAPTER THREE

The Counselor as a Co-worker

COFFEE, TEA, OR . . . COUNSELING

You have realized for some time that Charles Underwood, a general science teacher at your school, is anticounseling. He has never referred a student to you and you've heard that he's been discouraging other teachers from recommending students for counseling. Yesterday he told a group of teachers that, aside from the physical education teachers, you have the easiest job in school. He is recognized as one of your school's leaders. You're concerned because he is beginning to pick up some faculty followers in this anticounseling campaign.

Today you walk into the faculty lounge at a time which also happens to be Mr. Underwood's planning period. He, and the several other teachers in the lounge, became very quiet as you walked in. Then, as you knew it would someday happen, Mr. Underwood directs his negative comments straight to you. "How many cups of coffee you had today?" he asks blatantly. "You must have a cast iron stomach. I was just telling the others how you counselors have got it made. You sit down there and maybe see eight to ten kids a day while we work with 175. You can get up and come down here when you damn well please." Before you can say anything, he continues. "And another thing, you want to know why I never send anybody to the guidance office. Well, it's because you'd never do anything except take sides against me. No teaching, no lunchroom supervision, no bus duty, no disciplining; what do you do besides drink coffee?"

It's obvious that you have poor rapport with Mr. Underwood. He and the other teachers are waiting for your response. What will it be?

YOUR SOLUTION

YOUR REACTIONS TO THE ALTERNATE SOLUTIONS

ALTERNATE SOLUTIONS

1. Don't argue in front of the other teachers. Tell Mr. Underwood you would like to discuss your role with him in the privacy of your office.

2. Defend your role as a counselor then and there.

3. Simply tell Mr. Underwood that he's got a lot to learn about guidance and counseling and walk out of the lounge.

4. Encourage him to talk more. Most likely he will talk himself right under the table and will end up by apologizing to you.

5. Shrug it off with a joke and seek him out later.

SECRET AGENT 008

Your work is interrupted by the school principal who closes the door and tells you that he has a problem and wants to discuss it with you. He has received several telephone calls (three different parents) about a particular teacher—Mrs. Bell, sophomore English. Apparently some students are using obscene language in class and making coarse remarks to girls while the teacher attempts to carry on a class discussion. There is a lot of whispering, laughing, and playing pranks.

The principal gives you a list of names. You recognize some of them. A few are now in a counseling group and in the last group session one of the boys was confronted as "being obnoxious in Mrs. Bell's class." Although you were focusing on the boy's behavior and his impact on others, you heard several snide remarks made about Mrs. Bell and her classes. You have the impression that the teacher is threatened, confused, and having problems working with the less motivated students. You had planned to stop by and talk with her, perhaps do some consulting, but things kept piling up and now it appears that problems are bigger than you expected.

It is clear that the principal wants you to help him by telling what you know about the boys and the teacher and do some snooping for him. He says, "We've got to find out more about this and do something about it. I want you to check into this matter for me."

What should you do?

YOUR SOLUTION

YOUR REACTIONS TO THE ALTERNATE SOLUTIONS

ALTERNATE SOLUTIONS

1. Tell him what you know in general, but make it clear that cover work is risky business in terms of your relationships with the teachers.

2. He's your boss so cooperate by checking things out.

3. Ask the teacher if you can observe and then consult with her and the principal together.

4. Call in some students from Mrs. Bell's class and get reports on the class.

5. Suggest that he call in some students and talk with Mrs. Bell. You need to stay out of it.

THE COUNSELOR IS UNDERSTANDING . . .
TOO UNDERSTANDING

Dale Small spoke with you about the trouble he was having in geometry class. He said he couldn't talk with his teacher, who always made him feel stupid. According to Dale, the teacher was not very helpful and ignored him when he asked questions. Because he was falling behind in the class, Dale wanted a transfer to another section. He also thought of dropping the class and starting again next semester with a different teacher. You had listened attentively, but no decision was made. You agreed to talk further about the matter at another time.

Later that same day, Mr. Green, Dale's geometry teacher, came to your office and said, "I hear you've been talking with Dale Small. He told me that you're going to transfer him out of my class. He probably said that I never work with him or answer his questions, and a whole bunch of other things, huh? Well, let me tell you a thing or two!"

Mr. Green went on to explain how he had tried to work with Dale but the boy didn't follow his directions. Dale's work was termed sloppy and careless. "He asks the same questions and is more interested in socializing in class than in getting his work done." Mr. Green emphasized that he saw counselors as people who handed out crying towels and always took the student's side against the teacher. He concluded by saying, "You never hear the teacher's story. You just let kids come in here and rip us apart. Besides, instead of listening to their complaints, you should send them to see us and let us work out the problems. I stay in my room after school every night and work with students. Dale hasn't been there one time this year, and I'll bet he didn't tell you that!"

What's your response?

YOUR SOLUTION

YOUR REACTIONS TO THE ALTERNATE SOLUTIONS

ALTERNATE SOLUTIONS

1. Tell Mr. Green that you did not agree to transfer the boy out of the class and that apparently a three-way conference is needed to straighten out the misunderstanding.

2. Tell Mr. Green that you can accept his being upset over the incident, but you think that your role is to try to understand the boy's point of view.

3. Tell Mr. Green that if Dale had perceived the teacher as understanding, then he wouldn't have had to come to the counselor to talk about his problem. You now see your job as helping the two to communicate more effectively with each another.

4. Explain that counselors realize that students complain about teachers and sometimes distort events beyond recognition, but one part of the counseling process is to help students to come to understand themselves better in certain situations by listening to them and not taking sides either for or against teachers.

5. Summarize the situation as best you can and tell Mr. Green that you will encourage Dale to meet with him to work things out.

6. Ask Mr. Green if he still wants to work with the boy under the circumstances. If he does, arrange a joint conference; if not, transfer the boy.

I SPY

Last Friday evening you attended a movie in a neighboring town and saw Mr. Hinkle, a first year social studies teachers, and Susie, one of your school's senior girls. You were sitting three rows behind them and, by their overt display of affection you sensed that it was a date arrangement. They did not see you.

One of the things, Mr. Smith, your principal, dwells on in the first meeting of new teachers is maintaining professional relationships with students.

You also oppose the idea of imposing your values on others; yet, you know you're a part of the school team and you wonder what your next move is. What will it be?

YOUR SOLUTION

YOUR REACTIONS TO THE ALTERNATE SOLUTIONS

ALTERNATE SOLUTIONS

1. First thing Monday morning, tell your principal what you saw.

2. Call in Susie and tell her that her dating Mr. Hinkle jeopardizes his future.

3. Forget the whole thing. They didn't see you and there's no harm done. What they do is their business.

4. Call in Mr. Hinkle and let him know that you saw Susie and him on Friday night.

5. Send an anonymous letter to Susie's parents, with a caution statement.

6. Say nothing, but keep an eye on them in school.

THE APARTMENT

Mr. Mitchell, a math teacher in your school, has in the past drawn undesirable attention to himself by, among other things, holding weekend student stag parties at his bachelor apartment. Several times you have passed his classroom, during his planning period, and noticed Mr. Mitchell and Jimmy Newman alone in the room. One day, while talking with Jimmy, he unexpectedly proclaims, "I think Mr. Mitchell's queer." As you and Jimmy continue to talk, he tells you that Mitchell has made some homosexual offers to him. What's your next move?

YOUR SOLUTION

YOUR REACTIONS TO THE ALTERNATE SOLUTIONS

ALTERNATE SOLUTIONS

1. Since Jimmy is a minor you should immediately phone his parents.
2. Phone the local police department for advice.
3. Call in Mr. Mitchell and confront him with Jimmy's accusation.
4. Since your school principal is responsible for the entire school, he should be told before anyone else and the matter should be turned over to him.
5. Call in Mr. Mitchell and Jimmy together for a conference.
6. Encourage Jimmy to report his story to the principal.
7. Say nothing at this time. Continue to explore matters with Jimmy through other meetings.

REBELS WITH A CAUSE

Washington Senior High School is located in a district where the majority of the students come from disadvantaged families and where the crime rate has increased over the past year. The school is receiving a lot of public attention. Because of unfortunate incidents early in the school year (e.g. a youth was shot, a drug pusher was apprehended in the hallway, and there were several on-campus fights) the school administration ordered the school grounds to be fenced, most doors to be locked, certain areas to be off limits to students, and issued new regulations for the restrooms and hallways.

You have been meeting with ten popular seniors in group counseling sessions. Yesterday the group decided to request a meeting with the principal to voice their complaints about the new rules and regulations. Today the meeting took place and you were taken completely by surprise. The usually open, friendly, and sympathetic principal became defensive when questions were asked, instead of listening, he interrupted and lectured. "You just don't understand the problem of running a school like this." A few students responded by saying they were in a prison and the school was dehumanizing them. As students asked for explanations regarding some procedures, the principal became increasingly upset and said the group was just trying to stir up trouble.

The meeting was a bitter disappointment to everyone. The students felt that they had not had the opportunity to voice their grievances and were dissatisfied. "It's impossible to talk with him" exclaimed one student. "The man's a tyrant, who cares nothing about students" said another.

As you left that meeting, the principal called you aside and said, "Hey, what are you trying to do? I thought we were all working together. But you let those kids sit down there in the guidance office and get all riled up about things that they know little about. All they want to do is make trouble and look like college radicals. I won't have it. This year is tough enough as it is and we need your help if we're going to see it through. I don't see encouraging students to rebel against school policy as being very helpful."

It was obvious that the principal was disappointed in you as a friend and counselor. Moreover, the students would want to meet again. Now what?

YOUR SOLUTION

YOUR REACTIONS TO THE ALTERNATE SOLUTIONS

ALTERNATE SOLUTIONS

1. Meet with the principal again and apologize for the outcome of the first meeting. Emphasize that you acted as an empathic listener and did not encourage rebellion.

2. Disband the group sessions since they are now under suspicion by the principal. Meet with students individually.

3. Continue meeting with the group. Take a more active role in helping the students develop new strategies for voicing their grievances to the principal.

4. Continue meeting with the group, but keep the focus away from complaints about school policy. Rather, use the experience to help students examine their feelings, behaviors, and outcomes in that situation.

5. Tell the students that the principal has made it clear that you can no longer meet with them and they will have to be understanding and put themselves in his shoes.

6. Tell the principal how surprised you were about the direction the meeting took and see if you can act as a liaison between principal and students for another meeting.

THE TEACHER NEXT DOOR

Mr. Overmeyer drops by your office and it's apparent that he has something important to say. "Look," he starts, "I don't want to cause any trouble for Henry, but you know, he's right across the hall in room 106 and sometimes he really lets go. You know what I mean? He really swears at those kids! He gets so upset with that homeroom of his. Can't really blame him though, he's got a lot of clowns in there. I thought I ought to tell you about it rather than the principal. Maybe you can help. I'm as tolerant as anybody but I think Henry ought to watch himself."

You thank Mr. Overmeyer and let him know you'll follow up. How?

YOUR SOLUTION

YOUR REACTIONS TO THE ALTERNATE SOLUTIONS

ALTERNATE SOLUTIONS

1. The following morning listen to Henry's room via the P.A. system and hear what's happening.

2. Call in some of Henry's homeroom students and check out Mr. Overmeyer's story before you do anything else.

3. Tell Mr. Overmeyer to talk with Henry and you stay out of it.

4. Ask the principal to send out a general memo to the faculty cautioning them against the use of profanity with students.

5. Call in Henry and ask, "How are things going?"

HAVE EMPATHY, WILL TRAVEL

Jerry Jenkins, a ninth grader at your school, has been in trouble with the police several times during the past two years. This morning you learned that Jerry had been temporarily interned in the local juvenile home. He has been charged with possession of marijuana.

You have been counseling with Jerry for the past six weeks and feel that you have developed a good relationship with him. Jerry has not done well in school but you thought that he was starting to do better. Last week the school psychologist gave Jerry several tests and this morning you received the results. The WISC yielded an IQ of 118.

You've attempted to tell Jerry about his potential and after receiving the intelligence test scores this morning you decided to drive out to the juvenile home and talk with Jerry about the results. Jerry was depressed but seemed pleased that you came to visit him and was also pleased with the results of his tests.

As you were leaving Jerry told you that Mrs. Swanson, a school social worker, had been to visit him that morning and that Dr. Wilkerson, the school psychologist assigned to your community school system, was coming to see him in the afternoon. Jerry was surprised at all the attention he was getting. So were you.

This afternoon you received telephone calls less than 15 minutes apart. Mrs. Swanson politely indicated to you that you were out-of-bounds in going to the juvenile home. She informed you that when a student is confined to a juvenile detention home it is her function to visit the student's home, talk with the student, and report back to the school. She told you that your job is to counsel students while they are at the school. She made an appointment to see you tomorrow.

Dr. Wilkerson was not as polite as Mrs. Swanson in telling you that you had overstepped your authority visiting Jerry. He was especially upset with the fact that you have interpreted the WISC for Jerry. He indicated that when he is called to a school to give a test, he expects to interpret it for the examinee. He also has an appointment for tomorrow.

You seem to have gotten yourself into a real jam with two of your pupil personnel colleagues. How will you handle this?

YOUR SOLUTION

YOUR REACTIONS TO THE ALTERNATE SOLUTIONS

ALTERNATE SOLUTIONS

1. Simply admit to both of them that you went beyond your role and function by going to visit Jerry.

2. Tell them both that going to visit Jerry and talking to him about test results were entirely part of your role and function and that you will continue to make such visits when your students are involved.

3. Sit down with the two of them and clarify your role and function. Have them clarify their roles to you.

4. You have nothing to defend. Let them talk—just be empathic.

5. Take the matters to the pupil personnel services director in the school system and let him straighten things out.

I'M WITH YOU, BUT . . . .

Your principal informs you that he has heard some rather unbelievable things concerning some of your group counseling activities.

He states, "Now, I'm all for these groups you've been running here. But, I've heard that there is a lot of swearing in these groups. I don't know how accurate the reports are, but you're working in a school setting and, since I'm responsible for the entire staff's activities, I don't want any swearing going on in any school related activity and that includes counseling."

Open communication without restriction to language is a part of your group counseling policy. How do you respond to the principal?

YOUR SOLUTION

YOUR REACTIONS TO THE ALTERNATE SOLUTIONS

ALTERNATE SOLUTIONS

1. You don't condone swearing, but allow it because you believe in a permissive discussion.

2. You apologize and say it won't happen again.

3. You say that you understand his position and in future meetings will not permit swearing.

4. Have a meeting with the principal to discuss the nature of the group counseling climate in order to justify your behavior.

5. Say nothing, but report this discussion to the groups and get their reactions.

MIRROR, MIRROR ON THE WALL . . .

You're the guidance director and Bill James is a new counselor who is meeting with the guidance committee for the first time. He says, "Too many of the teachers treat their students as if they were objects. For example, Dale Rigness wanted to talk with his shop teacher about a very important personal problem and the teacher said he wasn't about to accept any excuses for late work. The teacher gave him some advice on how he could do better and told him how tough he had had it in school. Dale was crushed and came to see me. I let him talk and just listened. Before long he was feeling better and much more interested in school than before. That's why I think teachers shouldn't try to counsel with kids. Rather they should send them to see us, after all, that's what we are prepared to do."

One of the teachers in the committee turns to another teacher and you hear her say, "Didn't I tell you, another one of the 'beautiful people.' Counselors think that they are the only ones who should work with kids on a personal basis because they alone understand their problems. They're too much!"

You're listening. Bill continues to explain why counselors are better trained to be more understanding, caring, and accepting of students. One of the teachers takes out a pencil and begins doodling, obviously tuning out Bill. The other looks at Bill and glares, with arms folded. You feel the need to do something, but what?

YOUR SOLUTION

YOUR REACTIONS TO THE ALTERNATE SOLUTIONS

ALTERNATE SOLUTIONS

1. Tell the group how you agree and disagree with what Bill is saying so that they will know where you stand on the issue.

2. Tell the teachers that there are, of course, many teachers who are capable of working with students' personal problems, but that some are not effective when they try to help, and many don't recognize their limitations.

3. Talk about the gripes teachers have regarding counselors and vice versa.

4. This is not a time for an encounter group. Get the committee to talk less about complaints and focus on a problem common to all. Talk to Bill later about establishing rapport with teachers.

5. Give Bill a clue that he is treading on dangerous ground.

I WANT A TRANSFER

Thomas Baldwin had worked in other school systems before. This was his first year in Newberry High School. He had a record of absenteeism in the past, but otherwise had good teaching credentials. He seemed likeable, was alert in staff meetings, and joined in the humor of teacher lounge conversations. He was always on time and hadn't missed any school days this year. So, it came as a surprise when a group of students met in your office and began complaining about Speech 101 with Mr. Baldwin.

Student 1: "You see, he never listens to your speeches. He just sits in the back of the room and goes to sleep."

Student 2: "Yeah, like yesterday. I was giving my speech—a good one too—and he drops off to sleep right in the middle of it. So I thought "to heck with it" and just sat down.

Counselor: Are you saying that Mr. Baldwin closes his eyes and doesn't say anything if you stop in the middle of your speech.

Student 2: "Yes! But, he more than closes his eyes, he actually goes to sleep."

Student 3: "That's right! When he's asleep you can do whatever you want. Some people actually leave the room and go do other things."

Student 1: "I can tell you this, if I get a low grade in that class, then I'm going to tell my parents just what's happening in that room."

Student 2: "I've already told mine."

Student 3: "I'd like to transfer to another class."

What do you do?

YOUR SOLUTION

YOUR REACTIONS TO THE ALTERNATE SOLUTIONS

ALTERNATE SOLUTIONS

1. Sneak down and observe the class. File your report with the principal.

2. Make a record of the complaints. Ask that you be kept informed when it happens so that you can make note of the day and time.

3. Call in Mr. Baldwin and tell him what you have heard.

4. Get the students to talk with Mr. Baldwin and voice their complaints to him.

5. Inform the Chairman of the English and Speech department and see if Mr. Baldwin is feeling well.

6. Encourage the students to talk with the principal after they have clarified their complaints with you.

THE COUNSELOR AS A
CO-WORKER

There is a famous story about a very successful high school football coach whose teams had won several state championships. The community came to expect winning seasons and enjoyed the recognition given to its school and players. One local critic said that the coach was successful because he had so many outstanding players to pick from and that anyone could be a winner with so much talent. When the coach retired, a successor was selected and it was expected that a winning tradition would continue. But to the new coach's misfortune the winning tradition suddenly came to a halt. Eventually state championships were no longer taken for granted in the community, but became a regular part of the seasonal speculation about the sport as other coaches came and went. Although there were many individual players who were outstanding and who later played on college and professional teams, the community has not won another championship since the old coach retired. In seeking an explanation, one person said that now all communities have better players. Another said that today's game is more difficult and that no one could expect to be as successful as before.

When the old coach was asked about the differences, he replied, "Being a successful coach means getting to know players, their capabilities and potentials, and encouraging each individual to work hard at his task in order to make every play run properly. It's a matter of working at teamwork and avoiding the pitfalls that prevent a squad from becoming a cohesive working unit." In general, all coaches are knowledgeable about their sport. If there is a difference between winning and losing, it lies not only with selecting and using players properly, but in meeting the challenge of helping individuals to learn to get along with each other and to work well together.

Many large companies and organizations have drawn upon the concept of teamwork to make them successful. Educational institutions are no different. As a counselor you will be an important member of an educational team. You will be assigned a position and asked to perform as agreed upon by the rest of the team. Whether or not you reach star status will depend on your ability and willingness to work. It will also depend on the help and cooperation of your coworkers—teachers, administrators, students, support personnel, and other specialists. You alone, an individual with a general background in guidance and counseling, cannot accomplish the complex and complicated educational goals that most schools have set for themselves.

The authors are aware of many schools today where counselors have alienated themselves from their coworkers. While most counselors recognize that cooperation and understanding between the faculty members is essential for a successful guidance program, sometimes a counselor becomes so involved in working with students, that he fails to take account of his rapport with the rest of the school personnel. In taking account, there are many pitfalls to guard against if a good working relationship is to develop between a counselor and his coworkers.

Perhaps the biggest pitfall, and the one where most problems originate between a counselor and his coworkers, is a breakdown in communication. What causes this communication breakdown? One cause may be the counselor's inability to explain his role to the rest of the staff. If you have a confused concept of your role and function, or feel that you cannot articulate your ideas to other members of the staff, then you can expect many problems to develop. The faculty's picture of a school counselor is largely based on your own perceptions of a counselor's role and the degree to which you can communicate and implement that role. If your school does not have a written guidance philosophy, which includes a description of a counselor's role and function, you will want to initiate the writing of one and ask the help of your school's guidance committee.

Many counselors have a problem because of a misunderstanding regarding confidentiality. Certainly most counseling relationships require privacy because of the self-revealing and intimate experiences that are sometimes related by the counselee to the counselor. Both the American Personnel and Guidance Association and the American Psychological Association have adopted codes of ethics which govern the ethical responsibilities of their members. The codes point out that personal material received in counseling becomes an entrusted communication and the nature of the counseling relationship imposes an obligation of confidentiality. On the other hand, it is also recognized that matters of confidentiality and of counselor ethics are extremely complex and many times can only be resolved when the unique circumstances of a specific situation are considered. There are limits to confidentiality since the counselor also owes allegiance to the institution which employs him, and also must respect the rights of society and the community. If the teachers in your school see you as a sponge that soaks up and withholds information, they might become skeptical as to whether or not you can be of service to them. "After all, we're working with the student too and are just as interested in his welfare as you are." This comment suggests that teachers want information that will be of help to them in their work with students. You will antagonize many professional people if you declare or imply that only counselors can hold certain types of information in confidence. You will want to share information with a teacher who has made a referral to you, but you need not violate the confidence of a counselee.

Most teachers will not ask you to reveal everything that was told to you by your counselees, but they will expect some kind of feedback that will help them to establish guidelines in working with particular students. In this case, you may find it helpful to generalize your impressions of the student, rather than to detail the information given to you. Information that is harmless in nature does not usually bind the counselor to confidentiality and can be shared with your coworkers. In any event, it is important that you assist teachers in the use of any information you provide them.

Another pitfall that frequently causes problems between counselors and their coworkers results because counseling is neither a teaching nor an administrative position. Your image is not always easy to discern and it is often affected by the particular school that employs you. In some cases counselors are paid more than teachers. This is not a favorable policy since it polarizes counselors and teachers. If counselors identify themselves with the administrative staff, then teachers rarely complain about the extra pay. Regardless if you align yourself more with the administration than with the teaching staff, you can expect teachers to wonder at times whether or not you quiz students in order to find out if they are doing a good job. Also, if you're seen as an administrator's assistant, teachers will expect you to discipline students and do other things an administrator generally does.

It is not uncommon for a few teachers on a school faculty to feel that counselors are privileged people, which can become a pitfall to any team. Some of your coworkers are going to think that you have the easiest job in the school. After all, you are not required to meet with classes each day, you have no particular course outline to follow, you don't discipline students, and you don't have to respond to the bell system or the schedule of classes that programs a teacher's life. In addition, it seems that you can go to the lounge whenever you please. For those teachers who have problems managing large classes, your work with small groups or individuals will appear particularly appealing. Some may even suggest that while they have difficulty managing a classroom they could be effective as a counselor because it's easier to work in a one-to-one relationship. As teachers come to know of your work and recognize that you have a limited amount of time to accomplish an unlimited amount of tasks they will no longer see you as a privileged character.

It is possible that you could work with another counselor who spends most of his time hiding behind paper, avoiding teachers and students, or spending too much of his time drinking coffee in the teacher's lounge. You will find in this case even more fuel added to a potential conflict. It is important to be aware of how your coworkers perceive you and your counseling colleagues. Unprofessional or irresponsible counselor behavior will often result in snide remarks that give evidence to a less than satisfactory coworker relationship.

If you view yourself as a psychotherapist more than a counselor, and spend most of your time in a closed office working with students who have "in-depth psychological problems," there is a chance that you will fail to gain the staff relationship that is necessary for a successful guidance program. Few things will turn a staff against you quicker than the implication that you are practicing the mysteries of psychotherapy. In fact, you will not be a trained psychotherapist working in a miniature health clinic. While most of your training and basic preparation was of a psychotherapeutic nature, you will never have the time to engage in long in-depth psychological encounters.

The basic orientation and work of the counselor itself can be a stumbling block with your coworkers. As a counselor, you will most likely be prepared to use approaches that are nondirective and which look carefully at the counselee's point of view. If you are like most counselors, you will attempt to develop a helping relationship by using methods that are, more often than not, less directive than those of teachers and administrators. For example, you will want to have time to establish yourself as an understanding listener, a person who encourages a student to talk about himself in an attempt to help that student gain personal insight into his behavior. In contrast, most teachers and administrators are oriented toward more expedient methods and more deliberate kinds of information and ideas. To many of them, counselors are too permissive, and they criticize counselors for not obtaining immediate changes or results with students. Research suggests that your coworkers will be more cognitively oriented than you and that they will tend to spend most of their time talking to students than listening to them, even when they tell you that they have been "doing a little counseling." The most informed teachers know that you are not an instant magician who can change attitudes and behaviors with a pep talk. The informed coworker recognizes that your contribution to the team is unique and will support a more permissive and less directive style when you feel it is appropriate.

Whose side are you on? This is a game and a dangerous pitfall that counselors should beware of, but your position of being neither an administrator, nor a classroom teacher makes it difficult to avoid. If you are not a secret agent for the administration, then to some you must be a nursemaid to problem students. Some teachers complain that counselors always side with students against teachers and that a counselor's primary purpose is to pass out crying towels. "Why don't you ever hear our side of the story" is a frequent complaint by many teachers. If you want to avoid these kinds of complaints then you will have to, on occasion, leave your office and seek out other school personnel and talk with them about your work.

One of the best ways to form a cohesive educational team with a guidance point of view and to avoid self-defeating pitfalls is to form an active guidance committee. Guidance committees meet periodically to clarify guidance objectives and important school issues. If a guidance committee is nonexistent, start by appointing one.

A guidance committee may consist of teachers, parents, students, and an administrator. If a written philosophy exists for your school you will need to review it from time to time with the guidance committee. Because there are so many activities that might capture your time, it is important to specify in writing those functions to which you will give high priority. Yet, even though a written philosophy exists, your coworkers will depend on you to communicate some of the more specific details of your job. In addition, the guidance committee can plan a guidance calendar, hear special student cases, help integrate guidance and the curriculum, assist in public relations, and facilitate team communication.

FOR FURTHER READING

Arbuckle, D. "Counselor, Social Worker, Psychologist—Let's Ecumenicalize." *Personnel and Guidance Journal* 46 (1967): 532-38.

Clark, C. "Confidentiality and the School Counselor." *Personnel and Guidance Journal* 43 (1965): 482-84.

Escott, S. "The Counselor-Teacher Relationship." *School Counselor* 11 (1963): 215-20.

Gibson, R. L. "Teacher Opinions of High School Guidance Programs." *Personnel and Guidance Journal* 44 (1965): 416-22.

Mindel, M. T. "The Role of the Guidance Specialist in the In-Service Education of Teachers." *Personnel and Guidance Journal* 45 (1967) 692-96.

Shear, B. E. "Teamwork in Personnel Services." *Counselor Education and Supervision* 1 (1962): 199-202.

CHAPTER FOUR

The Counselor as a Manager

A 25 HOUR DAY

When you arrived at work this morning your counseling colleague gave you a paper and said, "I wrote this — it's about yesterday."

6:15 a.m. The alarm goes off! The concert was over at 9:15, but I just couldn't get away from Mrs. Wyman, John's mother.

6:30 a.m. "Look, I'm sorry to bother you at home and so early, too."

7:30 a.m. Parent conference (they have to be to work by 8:30.)

8:00 a.m. "Hey, Mrs. Walter's substitute is going to be late, will you babysit up there for a little while?"

8:20 a.m. Phone rings—"Yes, Swan Avenue is in the new boundary for North Side High." "I understand how you feel Mrs. Brown—"

8:45 a.m. "Ok, ok, you're sick. I'll call your mother."

8:50 a.m. "Juvenile aid officers again?"

9:50 a.m. "Mrs. Gate, we have these three boys that have been referred for testing. When can you get to them?"

9:55 a.m. Wow! Where are all these class schedule changes coming from?

10:15 a.m. I got a chance to do some individual counseling (sure wish I could do more of this).

11:20 a.m. Not lunchtime already! (Joe and I have got to get some help with the cafeteria.)

12:10 p.m. "You're a freshman—what are you doing in the cafeteria during the tenth-grade lunch period?"

1:00 p.m. This lunch looks good today. (The P.A.) "Yeah, I'll be right there." "You say you fell while high jumping?"

1:30 p.m. Phone rings—"What foreign language should Mary take next year if she plans to enter Parkview School of Nursing?"

1:40 p.m. Late to my counseling group again! (I wish I could run a couple of these each day instead of two a week.)

3:05 p.m. Oh no, student council meeting and facility advisory meeting at the same time—

6:00 p.m. "I'm sorry to call you at home, but Bill brought home an F today and—" (I must get an unlisted number.)

It was a hectic day for Bill, but not unusual for either of you. You and Bill realize that you're not doing enough of what you are best prepared to do—counseling. How can you change this situation?

YOUR SOLUTION

YOUR REACTIONS TO THE ALTERNATE SOLUTIONS

ALTERNATE SOLUTIONS

1. List your priorities and refuse to do those things that don't have high priorities.

2. Talk with the principal and clarify your role and function.

3. Ask for a transfer to a school that will use the services of a counselor and not expect a jack-of-all-trades.

4. Ask for time at the next faculty meeting and clarify your role and function for the entire staff.

5. Call on one of your senior counselors to talk to your principal about your role and function.

THE DETECTIVE

For the last three weeks the school restrooms have been a mess. Seldom does a day pass when the plumbing is not clogged and the maintenance staff must be called to clean up. It's suspected that a student, or a group of students, is deliberately creating the inconvenience. The principal has asked teachers to be more alert while on hall duty in an attempt to solve the mystery.

Randy Sullivan became your counselee several weeks ago. He is a marginal student, but seems to be getting along with his teachers and is passing most of his subjects. Some teachers have said that Randy would probably have dropped out except for your encouragement and supportive counseling. He didn't trust you at first, but now you seem to have his confidence and a good counseling relationship.

One day when Randy was meeting with you he said in passing, "By the way, you know the problem that they're having with the restrooms? Well, everyone thinks it's funny, especially to see old Jones (the janitor) dragging his mop down the hallway and then playing detective the rest of the day. Have you seen him? (He laughs.) All they are doing is flushing their lunch sacks down the toilets and some of them plug up. Then the next poor soul comes in and swoosh, all over the floor." (He laughs.)

Your curiosity is aroused and you want to ask who are "they," but before you say anything, Randy continues, "That dumb Jerry Waldin . . . he'll do anything. He's going to get caught, it's just a matter of time. I told him he's crazy, but he says everyone is getting a kick out of it. Hey, by the way . . ." Randy switched the topic to another point of interest. You talked a little more and then Randy left for class. You think it's great that Randy is finishing school, but you also reflect on the information that you have received. The mystery is solved. At least part of it. At least for you. But what now?

YOUR SOLUTION

YOUR REACTIONS TO THE ALTERNATE SOLUTIONS

ALTERNATE SOLUTIONS

1. Assume that Randy wanted you to know and pass on the information. Inform the principal that Jerry Waldin is one source of the problem.

2. Say nothing to anyone else. "It's just a matter of time . . ."

3. Tell the principal that lunch sacks might be clogging the plumbing system, but mention no names.

4. Call in Jerry Waldin and confront him about his part in the situation, without revealing your source of information.

5. Call back Randy and tell him that you feel uncomfortable with the information that he gave you. Ask him what might be done.

6. Encourage Randy to confront Jerry Waldin and others with being more responsible citizens.

7. Call in the janitor and give him a few clues.

NOT OUT OF MY CLASS . . .

Scheduling counseling appointments in your school has become a problem—there are no studyhalls. There can only be limited meetings before and after school because so many students are dependent on bus transportation. It seems that your only approach is to call students out of scheduled classes. Some teachers cooperate more than others and it doesn't take you long to identify them. Recently, one teacher said, "Look, I want to help out. I think Marty would benefit from group counseling, but how about using other classes too—like Pearson's class?"

Mrs. Pearson's 15-year reputation as a math teacher is enviable. She is well-organized, expects and receives good work from her students, and many have given her credit as the teacher who most helped them to understand math. She also has the reputation of running a "tight ship." She dislikes class interruptions and has embarrassed students with her comments when they have been late or had to leave class early. She explains, "They need to be in class if they are going to keep up. And, I don't expect to hold special sessions for those who aren't in class when they should be. Besides, some like to get out of class so that they won't have to take tests when they are first given."

You're convinced that Marty would benefit from a few group counseling sessions. He feels that he can keep up in math, but it involves missing Mrs. Pearson's class once a week if the group is to meet. What are you going to do?

YOUR SOLUTION

YOUR REACTIONS TO THE ALTERNATE SOLUTIONS

ALTERNATE SOLUTIONS

1. There's no use penalizing the student. Save your time and energy and make arrangements with cooperative teachers.

2. Cancel the group plans and meet with Marty individually at another time.

3. Tell Mrs. Pearson that your work is important, too, and explain the reasons why Marty needs counseling at this time.

4. Inform Mrs. Pearson that you plan to have Marty excused from class, and if she penalizes him, you will take the matter to the principal.

5. Tell the principal that Mrs. Pearson is not cooperating with the guidance department and that a conference needs to be held in order to straighten things out.

6. Draw up an agreement or contract with Mrs. Pearson and other teachers involved, which excuses the student for a specified day of the week and period of time. Teachers are not to give tests or penalize students for missing class. The contract is renegotiable at the end of the time period.

UNDERSTANDING THE MISFITS

You are the faculty adviser for the student council at Brooker High School. This year's student council, the only student government organization at Brooker, has been involved in several creative and innovative projects. Most recently it has been deeply involved in the planning of guidance activities for the entire student body.

During this week's meeting the council initiated the idea of having a panel of local college students appear before the entire student body at an assembly. The panel would consist of three college students: one from a local commune known as the "Candle People," a drug user, and a member of a radical student organization.

You let them know that you can understand their desire for this type of panel, but that it is doubtful that the principal and the faculty members on the guidance committee will approve. They are adamant. What's your solution?

YOUR SOLUTION

YOUR REACTIONS TO THE ALTERNATE SOLUTIONS

ALTERNATE SOLUTIONS

1. Suggest they counterbalance the panel with a student-minister, a member of the Students Against Drug Abuse, etc.

2. Go ahead with the panel discussion, and if questions arise, be ready to justify your reasons for having such a program.

3. Help the students to clarify their program proposal, and suggest they present it to the principal and guidance commitee.

4. Tell them that this type of program is not within the objectives of your guidance program and refuse to back them.

5. Suggest that they look for films to portray the ideas rather than a panel discussion.

TO SEE OR NOT TO SEE

You're attending a counseling staff meeting. Six counselors from your school are present and also the district coordinator of guidance, who is asking the group to think of how they are using their time with students. It has been school policy that students be interviewed at least once each year by their counselors, in addition to program planning. However, some counselors feel that counseling should be administered on a more limited basis, perhaps with counselors seeing only those students who volunteer to come in. Each counselor is asked to express his opinion to the question: who should meet with the counselor for counseling and when? What's your response to the district coordinator?

YOUR SOLUTION

YOUR REACTIONS TO THE ALTERNATE SOLUTIONS

ALTERNATE SOLUTIONS

1. "Not all students need to see the counselor for counseling. Those that want to will initiate a request to meet for a conference."

2. "All students should meet with the counselor at least once each year because some need help but do not seek it."

3. "Identify a small number of students who need your help most and work primarily with them. See others on a voluntary basis only."

4. "See students only on a teacher or self-referral basis."

5. "Increase group counseling activities and see all students either in a group or individually."

THE AGE OF ACCOUNTABILITY

The school district is operating on a tight budget and the new school board members plan to investigate all aspects of the educational program in your district to eliminate all the "frills." The principal has talked with you about some comments made to him by board members. One board member suggested that if counselors were eliminated, more teachers could be hired, and this would reduce the classroom ratio. Another asked "How do we know if what they do has any effect?" Another said, "I want to know how much I am paying per interview and what effect the counselor has?"

Today, your principal comes to your office and says that the superintendent wants every school principal to investigate and report to him on every part of the school curriculum. He states, "This is the age of accountability and we want each department, including counseling and guidance, to show its value. You have one semester to justify the existence of your program." What are you going to do?

YOUR SOLUTION

YOUR REACTIONS TO THE ALTERNATE SOLUTIONS

ALTERNATE SOLUTIONS

1. Conduct action research, with an emphasis upon the operational procedures used by the guidance staff.

2. Send a followup questionnaire asking former students to evaluate the guidance program.

3. Present individual case studies.

4. Obtain testimonials from current students, teachers, and parents.

5. Just have faith and hope that the program speaks for itself.

THE COUNSELOR AS A
MANAGER

There is more to a school's guidance program than just counseling, and counselors generally prefer that someone else take care of administrative details so that they can do what they have been trained to do. However, unless someone assumes the responsibility for organizing and coordinating the guidance program, the work of the counselor is in jeopardy. When counselors ignore basic administrative procedures, they quickly learn that someone else will make decisions for them concerning the guidance program. Unfortunately, this rejection of administrative concerns by counselors creates additional problems which detract from their effectiveness.

Much of a school counselor's preparation is aimed at assisting him to relate to students. Top priority in counselor education programs is given to helping relationships, individual and group counseling procedures, and tests and their interpretation, sometimes at the expense of learning administrattive procedures. Consequently, beginning counselors often assume that they will step into an existing, well-organized guidance program. In most cases, however, the reality of the situation will call for the new counselor to assume active leadership. Beginning counselors should be the most up-to-date professional in the school regarding new techniques and innovative guidance approaches; and, therefore, they should willingly assume the major responsibility for the management of the guidance program.

What will be your professional role as the manager of a guidance program? As a counselor concerned with management you will focus on the following areas: (1) counseling and related activities, (2) integration of the guidance program into the total school program, and (3) trends in management.

COUNSELING AND RELATED ACTIVITIES

A critical problem in management is the use of counselor time. Unless your time is used wisely, there will be little time for counseling. Either by default or through the exercise of choice inevitably you will establish priorities. First priority is usually given to the counseling function. At least two-thirds of your time should be made available for one-to-one and/or group counseling relationships. The rest of your time should be used for the study of students, guidance activities, research, or in-service consultation with teachers and others.

Many of today's counselors find their counseling time and talents dissipated by noncounseling duties. For example, most guidance offices have come to include an information center where the counselor or a guidance worker maintains occupational files, college brochures and catalogs, local employment listings, and scholarship information. Consequently, some counselors have fallen into the trap of collecting and distributing information as their most important function.

The establishment of a Career and Educational Information Center in your school library will save you time and energy. Educational, vocational, and personal-social information should be an important part of every school library. With the help of your school librarian, you can eliminate the image of the counselor as dispenser of information and establish yourself in a role that is more educationally and psychologically oriented. After a student has browsed through materials in the library and collected ideas, the information becomes a vehicle for counseling. While not all counseling interviews will follow this approach, encouraging student to use services that are already available frees your time for more counseling.

For several years counselors were seen as specialists in testing. For the most part, the basic testing program of your school will be coordinated and administered by a district specialist. It will be his responsibility to disseminate the testing information to teachers and administrators, while you will serve as a consultant to them. This enables you to give more time to the counseling function. On occasion, you will probably administer some individual tests. Preferably, you should use the services of a psychometrist for individual testing. Some school districts are now training volunteer personnel from the community to administer various tests. This enables the counselor to spend more time talking with students individually and in groups about the test results. It is possible that one of your colleagues will show a keen interest in testing and ways in which the test results can be used to help students. In this case, the testing program within the school—administration and interpretation—might be exclusively conducted by the counselor. It does not seem to matter whether the person who administers the test counsels the student. In addition, this situation draws upon the strengths and interests of the counseling staff, and gives the most time for each to do his thing.

There are other organizational procedures which are of value and enable you to give more attention to high priority functions. To work with students in groups, large and small, has been proven to be effective and is economical in terms of time. You may need to establish periods of time during the day or week when you work with students and other activities are not permitted to interfere. For instance, if you believe that you must counsel groups of underachievers, then set aside a specific time each week for that purpose. In addition, you will find that a guidance calendar, both yearly and weekly, is an essential component of your program. A carefully planned guidance calendar allows you to plan ahead, give recognition to important functions, and inform others as to the activities taking place in your program. Finally, support personnel are valuable not only in terms of clinical assistance, but in the performance of routine guidance duties, and should be recruited and trained by you and the other counselors. A well-prepared paraprofessional who is effective with students and faculty can give you additional time for professional activities.

INTEGRATION OF THE GUIDANCE PROGRAM INTO THE CURRICULUM

If the individual student is to obtain satisfaction from his school experiences, it is important that the societal purposes and objectives of the school be kept in mind. In a school where teachers have a guidance point of view, where they are concerned with the development of the whole child, students will see school as a positive experience.

One method of utilizing teachers in guidance is through a homeroom program. The homeroom should be more than just a base for students to touch each day. A homeroom which involves students, teachers, and the counseling staff in organizing, planning, directing, and evaluating can become the hub of a guidance program.

Special consideration should be given to how students are assigned to a homeroom. An especially important criteria for placement is that students be assigned to a teacher whom they do not have for a subject matter class. Students are much more apt to discuss personal topics and problems with a homeroom teacher who holds no jurisdiction over them regarding grades. Teachers also feel more relaxed under this arrangement. The traditional passing out a handbook developed in the confines of the guidance office to the homeroom teachers, and expecting them to hold guidance discussions around some of the outlined units is not usually effective. Rather, students along with the teachers and the guidance office should be in charge of planning homeroom guidance activities.

Through in-service programs, teachers, students, and others can learn the basic dimensions of a helping relationship and some fundamental procedures which create a good learning climate. As teachers and students put guidance procedures into practice during a homeroom program, they learn to better understand and relate to one another. The inevitable effect is an improvement in the learning atmosphere in the classroom and school.

Guidance is interwoven within the curriculum and both are vital aspects of the total educational process. As the coordinator, or manager, of the guidance program you will have an opportunity to assist and offer leadership to the school's staff in guidance functions and activities within the curriculum. Through your leadership the guidance and counseling process can be realized as an integral part of each school day.

TRENDS IN MANAGEMENT

It is not our purpose to go into the details of the organization and administration of a guidance program. Other books have been written which are directed specifically to this topic.

In years past the guidance program existed as a subdivision of a group of general administrative services in the school setting. However, the trend is for the guidance department to develop its own administrative lines and functions, while achieving a distinct position in the organizational structure of the entire school program. Most schools are now large enough to employ more than one counselor. It is important that the counseling staff organize itself into a department, perhaps with an elected chairman. The department should meet at least once a week to consider special cases, weekly events, guidance committee activities, and review current approaches and techniques being used in the program, as well as innovations. Many times new ideas are met with resistance and must be worked through by the staff.

One new trend which you and your colleagues will want to explore is automation. While automation has not been as extensive in education as in industry and business, it is beginning to come of age in the schools. To begin with, most equipment has been designed for industry and has had to be adapted for use in the schools. Moreover, the equipment is expensive and because of rapid changes and new developments in the equipment, some school systems are reluctant to invest in it. Perhaps more important, however, is that the schools are tradition-oriented and change in any school system is slow. At the present time, only a few isolated schools have been able to take full advantage of automated systems.

Still, the impact of automation does affect the school and will eventually revolutionize the role of the counselor. It affects the counselor in at least two ways. It can free the counselor of routine guidance duties that are time-consuming and which detract from the goal of working individually and in groups with students. For example, hand recording materials that are usually included in a student's cumulative record — standardized test scores, grades, anecdotal reports, personality inventories, family background, medical information, and extra curricular activities — has been a burden to the counselor. Such routine clerical work not only lowers morale, but can result in omissions, errors, and eventually skepticism as to the value of using cumulative records.

Now data processing procedures enable the school to record pupil information automatically and efficiently. Automated duplication increases the availability of records and encourages teachers and counselors to use the information. In addition to helping make the program more effective and efficient, automation has some implications which are still to be explored. Computer-assisted counseling, perhaps computerized counseling, is an innovation that is now beginning to appear.

Because schools have been in existence for many decades, the role of teacher and administrator has been clearly defined. Guidance and counselors programs received the major impetus during the last decade and are still struggling to clarify theory, role, and function. Counse rs now know what is needed if the school program is to be personalized. But, many times they are frustrated in their efforts because they have failed to grasp the importance of being responsible for managing their profession, their programs, and their roles.

FOR FURTHER READING

ASCA. *The Role of the Secondary School Counselor.* Washington, D. C.: APGA Publication Sales, 1968.

Bentley, J. C. *The Counselor's Role: Commentary and Readings.* Boston: Houghton Mifflin Co., 1968.

Blocher, D.; Dustin, R.; and Dugan, W. *Guidance Systems.* New York: Ronald Press, 1971.

Hummel, L.; and Bonham, S. J. *Pupil Personnel Services in Schools: Organization and Coordination.* Chicago: Rand McNally & Co., 1968.

Kowitz, G. T.; and Kowitz, N. G. *An Introduction to School Guidance.* New York: Holt, Rinehart and Winston, 1971.

Roeber, E. C.; Walz, G. R.; and Smith, G. E. *A Strategy for Guidance.* Toronto, Canada: Macmillan & Co., 1969.

Shertzer, B.; and Stone, S. *Fundamentals of Guidance.* Boston: Houghton Mifflin Co., 1966.

CHAPTER FIVE

The Counselor and the Community

HAIR

Sixteen-year-old Ralph Petri, son of a psychology professor at a local university, has been sent to your office repeatedly because of his shoulder-length hair and his bizarre clothes. Several teachers have complained that Ralph doesn't conform to the dress code, and your principal has turned Ralph over to you with the comment: "Counsel this kid."

Yesterday you spoke to Ralph regarding his conforming to the dress code. Today, an irate Dr. Jerome Petri walks into your office and emphatically states: "Why do you people view maturation and development as simply a process of adjusting to the great society? Do you have to encourage the phenomenon of assumed similarity? I can understand these restrictive ideologies being advocated by your teachers and the principal, but I'm surprised at your actions. You're supposed to be a counselor. Why should all students make the same life choices and look like robots? My son's hair and dress are his concern, not yours." Now what?

YOUR SOLUTION

YOUR REACTIONS TO THE ALTERNATE SOLUTIONS

ALTERNATE SOLUTIONS

1. Apologize. Agree with him, but say you're just doing your job.
2. Tell him you were doing "reality counseling" with Ralph.
3. Refer Dr. Petri to the principal.
4. Call a case conference where the Petri family and Ralph's teachers are present.
5. Encourage Dr. Petri to talk and then introduce another of Ralph's problems.
6. Ask the guidance committee to reconsider the dress code.

THE CENTER

In the past your community offered little in the way of weekend recreation for high school students. Through your leadership and hard work a weekend center for students was recently established. A local church cooperated by offering its basement as a meeting place, and you've been serving faithfully as one of several chaperones.

The youths gather in the church's basement on Friday and Saturday nights. The majority of teenagers who attend are from your school. The students are constantly talking about the different singing groups that are to appear and seem excited about the recreational center. You've actually been doing quite a lot of inadvertant counseling during your rap sessions at the center. Many of the contacts you've made there proved helpful in counseling sessions at school.

Most recently some dropouts have been causing problems at the center. They sometimes smell of alcohol, and there has been quite a lot of unaccounted for damage to the church basement. Generally, they have left the premises when asked. However, this past Saturday night a large-scale fight broke out and the church basement was almost destroyed. To top it off, some students from your school were smoking pot in the restrooms.

The minister of the church, along with three of the church elders, walked into your office this morning and stated that the center would be closed if there were any more reports of fighting or drug use on the premises. You realize the importance of the center and want to see it remain open. What can you do?

YOUR SOLUTION

YOUR REACTIONS TO THE ALTERNATE SOLUTIONS

ALTERNATE SOLUTIONS

1. Appoint a student committee to investigate the problem.

2. Arrange for plain-clothesmen to keep the undesirables out of the center.

3. Arrange for a meeting with the leaders of the group responsible for problems.

4. Require everyone attending the youth center to show proof that they are in school.

5. Have the minister speak to a school assembly regarding conditions necessary for keeping the center open.

HARD LIVER

In your second semester of counseling (in a middle class suburban high school) you have become well acquainted with several parents and have been invited to a few Saturday night parties in the community. This week you accepted an invitation to one of these parties.

It's Saturday evening and you're attending the large party given by the Wallaces, whose son John has been in to talk to you about college, but you hardly know him.

You thought that you would be extremely uncomfortable at the Wallace's party. However, you look around and see some familiar faces among the group, and it appears that you may yet enjoy yourself. Mr. and Mrs. Wallace are cordial and tell you that they have several parties a year and that they generally invite at least one of John's teachers to each party. You feel bad, but say nothing. A short time later you walk up to the bar and Mrs. Wallace offers you a drink while she mixes herself one. You decline and ask for a coke. Mrs. Wallace, in a serious tone, states; "I'm really glad to see that you don't drink. We had a party a few weeks ago and Mr. Coker (your fellow counselor) turned out to be a real swinger. He really drinks and swears a lot. I understand he uses foul language when talking with boys. I always thought that teachers, and especially counselors, should set good examples for today's youth. Don't you agree?" What now?

YOUR SOLUTION

YOUR REACTIONS TO THE ALTERNATE SOLUTIONS

ALTERNATE SOLUTIONS

1. Tell Mrs. Wallace that you will talk to Mr. Coker about his behavior.

2. Defend your colleague's behavior then and there.

3. Tell Mrs. Wallace that it is unethical for you to talk about your colleague and say nothing more.

4. It's going to be a long night, smile, and switch to scotch and water.

5. Suggest that a persons private life may not alter his counseling effectiveness.

6. Suggest that Mrs. Wallace talk with Mr. Coker, if she is concerned.

INDIVIDUAL VS. SOCIETY

You have been asked to speak to your PTA regarding counseling and you conclude with the following: "So, in closing, I want to emphasize that the concepts of counseling may vary from educator to educator. Yet, as a profession, counseling was developed to meet certain societal needs. School counseling in particular was the outcome of the concern for the individual, his rights to freedom of choice, and the opportunity to develop his unique potential. This focus on the individual may at times pose a problem between the needs of society and those of the individual. However, as far as I'm concerned, the individual comes first, and that is what this country is about. Thank you."

After you finish your speech, a man stands during the question and answer period and asks:

"Counselor, are you telling us that the interests of the individual student should come before the interests of the majority? Doesn't that go against everything our American democracy stands for? How can you separate individuals from society when individuals make up society?

What's your answer?

YOUR SOLUTION

YOUR REACTIONS TO THE ALTERNATE SOLUTIONS

ALTERNATE SOLUTIONS

1. Smile and move on to the next question.

2. "Sir, the counselor does have certain responsibilities to society, but never at the expense of the individual."

3. "I hear you saying that you disagree with me. Would you elaborate on your point, please."

4. "My job is not to institutionalize, but to individualize."

5. Make a few brief comments, but avoid urguing. Ask the man to talk with you later.

THE EMPLOYMENT AGENT

The phone rings. It is Mr. Prentice, a local businessman, who wants some information about some boys in your school. It seems that Mr. Prentice is trying to decide who he might hire to work in his warehouse. He reads three names to you: Frank Bailey, Joe Hoyt, and Bob Dykes.

Frank Bailey is a good student who has a pleasing personality. He applies himself to his studies and also finds time to be involved in school clubs. He told you once that he wanted a job in order to save money for college. He said that a scholarship would also be needed if he were to attend college because money was not available from the family budget. There is no question in your mind that Frank is a highly motivated boy who knows what he wants and is willing to work for it.

You're not familiar with the second name, Joe Hoyt. However, the name Bob Dykes brings a clear picture to your mind. Bob is frequently on the absentee list, and you've been asked to talk with him about his absences and suspected truancies. He said that he wasn't interested in school and that this probably contributed to his "little illnesses." He does poorly in academic subjects but received A grades in woodshop classes where his projects were considered among the most outstanding in school. One teacher indicated that Bob could be a better student in all his subjects, but that he had to shift for himself because of family problems, and this lessened his interest in school. He doesn't dress as well as other students and once told you that he would like a job in order to buy some clothes and a motorcycle. Another teacher told you that Bob had a great deal of potential, but he needed to associate with a different group of boys who were more interested in school.

Mr. Prentice said he was impressed with all three boys thru brief interviews. He found his decision a difficult one because he knew all three wanted a job, and said he also likes to help deserving young people who are responsible workers.

Mr. Prentice is waiting.

YOUR SOLUTION

YOUR REACTIONS TO THE ALTERNATE SOLUTIONS

ALTERNATE SOLUTIONS

1. Tell him that you are not in a position to reveal information from school records. (Don't get involved in the employment business.)

2. Tell him that you will furnish him with what information you can. Using their folders, be objective, and try not to slant the report in any boy's favor.

3. Tell him that Frank Bailey is probably a good bet. Bob Dykes is a high risk based on school behavior, and that you don't know the other boy.

4. Tell him that although Bob Dykes' school record is not very good you think he needs the job more than the others, and it might help him become a more responsible person.

5. Tell him that you don't have enough information on the boys to be of much help in what he is asking; let him assume full responsibility for whom he hires.

THE COUNSELOR AND THE COMMUNITY

In years past people in a community would meet at the school to form picnics, observe national holidays, hold annual celebrations, and join in other types of local communal festivities. The school was a central and important part of the community. As time passed communities became larger and more complex and schools followed a similar pattern. For many people schools became giant monsters that consumed the taxpayers' dollars while taking over almost total responsibility for the education of the community's children. As society became more complicated, people limited their focus to their immediate family and became less interested in school and local activities. Thus, the school became just a place where parents sent their children each day to become prepared for the world of work. Consequently, only a few parents continued to retain an interest in the school progress. More and more parents came to rely on the professional judgment of educators and were content to be only generally informed on important issues, such as school budget votes.

School programs are constantly changing to meet the needs of the present and educators are generally neglectful in communicating these changes to the community. Sometimes changes occur so rapidly that some of today's parents would have difficulty in passing the routine examinations taken daily by their children. Some parents complain that they are not able to help their children with homework since curriculum has become so complex. Still other parents refuse to recognize the inevitable changes taking place in society and frequently complain that schools try to do too much for children and should return to the basic three R's. Others are unable to see the importance of preparing students for tomorrow's world, and frequently criticize and minimize the efforts of educators. There are, of course, many individuals in a community who will consistently provide the support that is necessary to sustain any successful school program. There are occasions when people choose sides. Many times misunderstandings and misinformation lead to the defeat of school budgets and result in a lack of critically needed financial support. Then there are communities which continually provide a vote of confidence for educators that makes them proud to be a part of the educational system.

One of the most important questions to ask yourself as a counselor is: what will the community expect of me? First of all, many people will be confused by your title "counselor." To some a counselor is a person who specializes in giving advice to individuals who are either in legal trouble, or who are experiencing personality problems. Many parents refuse to allow their child to see a counselor because counseling indicates to them and others (which may be the crux of the matter) that their child deviates from the norm, or is in some kind of difficulty. Some parents are threatened and feel that they are not doing an adequate job in raising their child if he is referred to a counselor. To meet with a counselor in some schools puts a stigma on the student and parents. In these situations it is not uncommon for a parent to ask, upon hearing that his child has met with a counselor, "Why do you need to see a counselor?" or "What did you do in order to be called in by the counselor?" These parents usually misunderstand the role of the counselor and lack information regarding the more positive aspects of your services to students in the school.

There are other types of parents who are glad to learn that you are seeing their child. However, some of them will perceive of you as a public servant who is required to collect information about their child and then dutifully report it to them and the teachers. A few parents may wonder whether or not you are invading their privacy, but for the most part it is generally accepted that your job is to organize information about students and accumulate it in a manner which will be helpful to parents, teachers, and others.

Some parents will expect you to be the friendly persuader. They may look to you as a knowledgeable collaborator in their plans for their child. That is to say, at times they will count on you to convince their child that their way of thinking is the correct one and should be followed. These parents recognize that students will turn to others and seek advice outside of the home, but they count on other adults to agree with their points of view. They expect the child to follow the path that has been laid out for him by them. For example, while they know that you will be involved in educational and vocational planning it is not uncommon to have some parents try to involve you in convincing their child that he should not date at a certain age, that he should run with a different crowd, should study more, be less demanding upon them as parents, or that he should try to get along better with his brothers and sisters.

Other parents will expect you to work with their child within a narrow framework, perhaps one that is traditionally related to limited academic areas. In this case, you will not be encouraged to discuss and explore feelings and attitudes as they effect the child's life choices. Rather, you might be asked by a particular child's parents to confine your discussions to intellectual growth and academic achievement.

On the other hand there will be those parents who will be less skeptical and suspicious of your work and expect you to be the person to contact and work with regarding a particular problem that their child may be having in school or in personal adjustment. If their child is not performing well in an academic subject, you may be the first person the parent will call in an attempt to make an appointment with the teacher. Some will come to complain about the teacher, a teaching method, or simply express their concern about their child's inability to apply himself.

There are also parents who might expect services that could go beyond your skills and preparation. For example, they could see you as a practicing psychotherapist who can resolve all kinds of personal problems, their own as well as their child's. During the academic school year most counselors will have an encounter with parents who begin talking about their children only to spend most of the time relating events and personal concerns in their own pattern of living, which are important, but only indirectly related to the purpose of a conference. In one instance, a mother came to talk with a counselor regarding her son's grades. Within a few minutes she began talking about her mother's ill health and how it had affected her. While this was undoubtedly related to the family living pattern, it seemed to skirt the issue of the boy's performance in school. There will be times when you will wonder whether you are to consult or counsel with a parent.

How will parents perceive you? The answer depends upon the community in which you work and how knowledgeable the community is about your program. However, there is some research evidence which indicates that parents will tend to view you as an individual who makes programs, handles school problems, and counsels students regarding careers. Research further indicates that they will tend to see you as more helpful in the areas of educational and vocational counseling and least helpful in personal, emotional, and social problems. Basically, parents see the school counselor as just another kind of teacher. This is particularly interesting in light of the fact that if you are like most counselors, you will view yourself as being most capable and effective in the area of personal counseling.

As a counselor you work for and serve many people. In addition to parents there will be other individuals and groups in the community who will have varied expectations of you. For instance, businessmen often turn to the school and request information regarding students whom they are planning to employ, to assure themselves that they should take a chance in employing a certain young person. Church groups will want your help in disseminating information for them and youth groups are always looking for people who are understanding and will request your services as a leader, or at least as a chaperone. There are people living in residential areas who will turn to you in hopes that you can convince students to stop destroying property, walking on lawns, or tipping over garbage cans.

What is going to be the role that you will play in satisfying the varied interests and expectancies that the people in the community will have of you? The different groups in the community will expect you to perform certain tasks. Some of these groups will complain bitterly if you do certain things, while others will voice complaints if you don't. Some groups in the community have more strength and support than others. Even though they may not serve the best interests of the school program they are often heard because their voices are loudest. Part of your job will be to keep your ear to the ground in order to hear all about facets of the community life. Eventually you will find a role that is comfortable for you in terms of your professional interests and preparation as well as fulfilling community expectations.

Another significant question is: what can a counselor expect from a community? In the first place, the community should be viewed as a vast resource area. At the very least, it should provide you with the opportunity to collect information which will be helpful in your work. In some cases, local businesses will provide you with brochures regarding career opportunities and offer to meet with students who are interested in pursuing a job in a particular business operation.

In addition to providing you with printed information, there may be agencies which will help you understand your students more effectively. For example, you will want to have a close working relationship with the welfare association, local juvenile authorities, local ministers, etc. In addition to expecting the Chamber of Commerce and local businesses to help you plan such activities as career days, job carnivals, or career fairs, these same groups can be of help in developing and organizing referral agencies and resource centers that are directly related to mental health. Some local businessmen will be among your greatest allies in helping you place students in jobs upon graduation.

Another way in which you can expect community help is through programs which will involve volunteer aides. Many people in community organizations can be of invaluable assistance to you in developing programs in specialized tutoring, big brothers, and work study programs. Through in-service training you can teach adults of local civic organizations to work in helping relationships with students. If you have the support of different civic organizations in your program, they will be eager to take an active part in guidance situations which you outline for them.

How will the community learn of your guidance and counseling program? The wise counselor does not take his position or program for granted. He recognizes that many members of the community have little knowledge of school programs and that it is his duty to inform them of the services that are available.

There are many opportunities in a community through which a counselor can make his program known. For example, early in the year you could present a program on guidance and counseling to your parent-teacher organization. Moreover, counselors in the past have tended to be too modest regarding the effectiveness of their programs. When something exciting and interesting is happening, it should be made known through such news media as television, radio, and newspaper. Encourage your school newspaper to carry a special news feature on guidance and counseling. This not only informs students, but the paper eventually makes its way to many homes to be read by parents.

It might be helpful for the guidance department to identify a project in public relations which would be carried out during the course of the academic year. Perhaps a special program could be developed and presented to local civic clubs or maybe on radio or television. It is a common fact that negative incidents usually receive more attention in the news than stories describing positive activities. Thus, if an unfortunate incident does develop, counselors find that advanced news items regarding positive elements of a guidance program are invaluable.

Public relations is a key to success—part of your job. Perhaps the first and most important public relations agents in your school are the students with whom you work. Every counselee automatically becomes a potential spokesman for you and your program. Most likely the way students perceive you will influence the way parents will see you. If a student goes home and describes how helpful you have been in his educational and vocational planning, parents are going to see you as an asset to their child's education. When a child goes home and explains how he is working out some difficulties in school with your help, parents tend to be grateful. Then there will be parents and local authorities who will learn that some students won't confide anything to them without having first talked to you. Such incidents as these suggest a counselor who is actively involved with the students. Counselors usually come into contact with someone in the community as a result of a crisis situation. At that time, the focus will be upon the immediate situation.

If your guidance program is primarily crisis-oriented, you will be involved with numerous discipline problems and often find yourself talking with students who are judged incorrigible or undesirable. Changes in behavior take time and you may find yourself working with only a few students over a long period of time. Consequently, it is possible that both students and community may come to view you as working only with those students who are experiencing problems. One of the best ways to avoid this limited view is to work with all types of students and let many others know what kind of work you are doing. For example, if you are running a series of rap sessions, which consist of a ramdom selection of individuals from the student body, this will let the community know that counselors do a lot of preventive guidance. Along the same lines, all counselors enjoy talking with intelligent, verbal students who are college-bound. Some enjoy the experience so much (or is it that they fear the others so much?) that those who have limited abilities are neglected. Don't be one of those counselors who contributes to advancing the advantaged at the expense of those who need the most.

When parents talk with a counselor they form many questions regarding the school. Even though they may have come to talk about their child, they sometimes pose questions which will require you to understand the total educational program offered in your school. They may question you about the educational philosophy, the school budget, or perhaps how the reading program is beneficial to their son. They may want to know why a teacher can use one method while another approaches the subject from a different angle. Because of your strategic position you will find yourself promoting the school program as it touches the life of each student. You will be involved in interpreting the total school program with its strengths and weaknesses.

Some members of the community will see you as a powerful authority figure who can talk students into and out of things. For example, you might someday get a call asking why your students continually take shortcuts over their lawn and shrubbery, or, you may hear from someone who says that a student has kicked over trash cans on the way home and your help is expected in finding out who the student is. Most important, if the student was identified, you could be expected to put him straight. In other words, there are going to be many days when you will be expected to be a sounding board, a complaint department, an information center, an investigator, and a miracle worker.

During the coming decade, schools will be asked to become more accountable to the community in terms of their services and outcomes. Counseling and guidance programs will not be exempt from scrutiny. In an effort to be more accountable, an emphasis on behavioral objectives has developed for school programs. Putting values, feelings, attitudes, and other counseling objectives into behavioral terms is not always easy. But, it is important for counselors to be responsible for their program and its outcomes. It is a time for counselors to be active professionals. Counselors must take their case to the community in advance and not wait until questioned as to their contributions to the educational program.

The authors recall one occasion where a counselor had made a presentation before a large group of community members, including many parents. There was a feeling of satisfaction as he was obviously well-received. The warm support was gratifying. However, one man spoke to the counselor and said, "I like your presentation. I'm not sure I understood all the things you were saying. In fact, I'm not really sure what it is that you do, how you do it, or even if you're effective at it; but, whatever it is, *keep it up.*"

For many years, counselors have enjoyed the support of the community because counseling and guidance programs make sense and have a personal appeal, but as we enter the age of accountability in the schools, you will want to aid members of the community in knowing what to expect from you and what you can expect from them.

FOR FURTHER READING

Bergstein, H. B. "The Parent and the School Counselor: An Emerging Relationship." *Vocational Guidance Quarterly* 13 (1965): 243-47.

Bergstein, H. B., and Grant, C. "Who Helps Children? Parents' Conceptions." *School Counselor* 12 (1964): 67-71.

Hoyt, K. B. "What the Counselor Has a Right to Expect of the School." In *Counseling and Guidance: A Summary View,* edited by J. F. Adams, 135-41. New York: The Macmillan Co., 1965.

Johnson, W. F., "The Public Relations Role of the School Counselor." Bulletin of the National Association of Secondary School Principals 44 (1960): 59-62.

3917

Moore, G. D., and Gaier, E. L. "Social Forces and Counselor Role." *Counselor Education and Supervision* 3 (1963): 29-36.

Muro, J. J. "Counselors Are the Men to Shape Your Public Relations." *American School Board Journal* 56 (1968): 19-20.

Shertzer, B., and Stone, S. "The School Counselor and His Publics: A Problem in Role Definition." *Personnel and Guidance Journal* 41 (1963): 687-93.